Called to Happiness

Called to Happiness

Where Faith and Psychology Meet

Sidney Callahan

ORBIS BOOKS
Maryknoll, New York 10545

Founded in 1970, Orbis Books endeavors to publish works that enlighten the mind, nourish the spirit, and challenge the conscience. The publishing arm of the Maryknoll Fathers and Brothers, Orbis seeks to explore the global dimensions of the Christian faith and mission, to invite dialogue with diverse cultures and religious traditions, and to serve the cause of reconciliation and peace. The books published reflect the views of their authors and do not represent the official position of the Maryknoll Society. To learn more about Maryknoll and Orbis Books, please visit our website at www.maryknollsociety.org.

Called to Happiness: Where Faith and Psychology Meet is a contribution to an interdisciplinary project on The Pursuit of Happiness: Scientific, Theological, and Interdisciplinary Perspectives on the Love of God, Neighbor, and Self, established by the Center for the Study of Law and Religion at Emory University and supported by a grant from the John Templeton Foundation.

Manufactured in the United States of America

ISBN 978-1-57075-918-5

Library of Congress Cataloging-in-Publication Data

Callahan, Sidney Cornelia.
    Called to happiness : where faith and psychology meet / Sidney Callahan.
        p. cm.
    Includes bibliographical references (p.   ).
    ISBN 978-1-57075-918-5 (pbk.)
    1. Happiness—Religious aspects—Christianity.   2. Christianity—Psychology.
3. Psychology and religion.   4. Psychology, Religious.   I. Title.

    BV4647.J68C35 2011
    241'.4—dc22
                                                2011008832

CONTENTS

Chapter 1

HAPPINESS NOW?

Are you happy? Are we happy? How much does happiness matter in the larger scheme of things? Since 1776 happiness has been an all-American question; the Declaration of Independence boldly states to the world that the pursuit of happiness is an inalienable, God-given right. This clarion call of the American Revolution put the pursuit of happiness right up there with the rights to life and liberty. No one could say that such commitments have faded away over the centuries. In 2009 President Barack Obama referred in his inaugural address to the "God-given promise" that "all are equal, all are free, and all deserve a chance to pursue their full measure of happiness."

America's interests in achieving a "full measure of happiness" can be said to be increasing and expanding. Recently I read a news report claiming that Americans think about happiness every day. Every day? While this statistic sounds a tad exaggerated, we can say that the country is experiencing a happiness boom. In the year 2000 some fifty books on happiness appeared, and by 2007 the number had increased to four thousand. By now, in 2011 if you go to Amazon.com and look under "happiness books," you can find forty-three thousand items listed. A Google search for "happiness studies and programs" produces some 261,000 citations. In the lists of available books, "how to become happy" guides alternate with intellectual and learned studies. One huge chunk of the advice books are self identified as "spiritual" in nature, and an even larger number are the products of psychologists claiming scientific authority and effectiveness for their work.

In more specialized academic circles another flood of publications, books, and hundreds of research articles and studies are devoted to happiness. Newly founded journals and professional conferences appear along with an innovative field known as the "science of happiness." At least one international center has been established in the Netherlands to provide a database for happiness studies, serving up fat bibliographies and a huge number of published resources from around the globe. On the Internet, a multitude of Web sites add information on all aspects of happiness.

Colleges offer new courses on happiness that are invariably well attended. One of Harvard's most popular courses is devoted to happiness, and the professor's class material is available in his new book, delivering "the secrets to daily joy and lasting fulfillment"; already it is a best seller. Happiness courses may assign reading from new and traditional works of philosophy, theology, literature, politics, and economics, but they are always certain to include the latest empirical social scientific and psychological research. Homework assignments and required happiness exercises are even more innovative features. Students may be asked to compose gratitude lists, send gratitude letters, perform acts of kindness, do savoring exercise, keep journals, or fill out different happiness questionnaires. Popular self-help guide books include similar exercise techniques.

Since happiness is of no small concern, academic scientific studies of happiness are quickly converted into active practical programs promising concrete results. Standard social scientific researches describing those who now are happy are converted into prescriptions for achieving future happiness. The market for such self-help guides is huge; even pessimists who are resigned to suffering want their children to become happy.

But can happiness be obtained as promised? That is the crucial and central question. The answer partly depends on how you define "happiness." "What is this happiness you seek?" You need to know what you're looking for before a hunt begins. The definition of happiness also determines the methods and strategies you should use. These kinds of fundamental questions have been examined and debated in philosophy and theology for thousands of years and still go on. Current happiness quests differ mainly in the addition of scientists and psychologists to the expedition. How do these new scientific seekers and explorers relate to the traditional seekers of happiness? In my judgment it seems clear that the newcomers do not aim to supplant other sources of wisdom, but rather to "supplement," "integrate and refine," and support the pursuit of happiness, using their own innovative tools and techniques. Unresolved issues still linger on the scene, not least of which is whether the new science of happiness should be seen as valid and reliable. With new claims, new debates begin and old ones resurface.

I have recently been privileged to experience a grand tour of the contested territories of current happiness disputes. I was invited to take part in an ongoing interdisciplinary working project on happiness that lasted for four years. The group met twice a year under the sponsorship of Emory University's Center for the Study of Law and Religion. The endeavor was called the Pursuit of Happiness Project (POHP). Our charge was to seek to understand the different approaches to happiness and their implications for the moral and theological well-being of the culture. The conference meetings and the ensuing publications were funded by the Templeton Foundation as part of its exploration of the relationships between science and religion.

Our working group included a philosopher specializing in ancient Greek thought, an evolutionary biologist, a lawyer or two, a rabbi, two scripture scholars (First and New Testament), and a clutch of theologians, ethicists, and psychologists with different and overlapping specializations. The religious scholars were from the Roman Catholic and Protestant traditions, and the psychologists represented clinical, developmental, positive experimental, and evolutionary psychology fields. (We used English as the lingua franca for cross-discipline communication.) Once solving the jargon problem, the group could argue more fiercely and at the same time mutually instruct each other. To add to the intellectual feast, outside experts on different dimensions of happiness came to speak to us. We heard what Thomas Jefferson meant by "the pursuit of happiness" and of Solzhenitsyn's spiritual experiences of happiness in the gulag. In a sobering presentation from British ecological expert Tim Jackson, we learned that a rethinking of the pursuit of happiness is desperately needed if the world hopes to avoid disaster from consumerism's depletion of natural resources. Jonathan Haidt, a leading psychologist in happiness studies, spoke on the evolutionary and socioreligious dimensions of happiness. These lectures and meetings were an interdisciplinary crash course on happiness, involving thousands of pages of reading plus assigned critical responses to others' papers and preliminary presentations and discussion of one's own chosen research project.

In the high-level sessions of back-and-forth argument it became clear, at least to me, that interdisciplinary research on happiness is just beginning on many fronts. As a critical human challenge with huge repercussions, human happiness is not an optional concern. Many more books, studies, and research projects will be pouring forth in the immediate future and in the long term.

At the beginning of our project the group plunged into difficult arguments over the definition of happiness that affect all later central issues, including practical and personal ones. In this book I also start with the definition problem. After wrestling with the challenge of defining happiness I conclude that our common culture can agree upon a robust and usable definition. For religious believers, however, more theological issues must be addressed, so I devote a chapter rather grandly to God and happiness, focusing upon Christian disputes over happiness. Religious differences over happiness in heaven and earth have another long history, and they are also still developing in provocative ways.

The newest and most controversial arguments over happiness may now be said to surround the multifaceted emerging science of happiness. These complicated issues are treated after the religious questions. In the discussion of empirical inquiries into happiness, disputes over the nature of science are inevitable. How, for instance, do value-based therapeutic interventions relate to supposedly value-free empirical research? The study of a human subjective experience like happiness presents special challenges for a science. The array of procedures, processes, attitudes, and behaviors that are being recommended as the scientific way to happiness need close analysis. Do they implicitly depend upon spiritual and religious principles and practices? Are they overlapping?

Certainly, traditional philosophical and religious paths to happiness and virtue require individual seekers to direct their thinking, emotions, and behaviors in a number of prescribed ways. Christianity and Buddhism both mandate certain practices if happiness is to be found. Becoming happy traditionally includes choosing good behavior, accepting certain beliefs, generating certain emotions, and avoiding destructive practices and thoughts. An applied science of happiness takes the same approaches, now backed up with the authority of scientific evidence.

Most recently an energetic new group of psychologists and social scientists have taken the lead in crafting a science of happiness that claims to use evidence-based techniques that work. A loosely allied positive psychology movement consists of a group of academically trained psychologists who differentiate themselves from their predecessors by vigorously affirming that humans possess innate strengths and manifold capacities for virtue, character, and positive emotions. These strengths and capacities can be intentionally activated and lead to becoming happier. Rather than have psychology concentrate on human pathologies, limitations, and suffering, the positive psychology movement wants to turn to the positive resources of humankind. They wish to challenge the powerful influence of happiness pessimists in their different incarnations. Happiness pessimists, whether secular or religious, doubt that human beings have the capacities to generate personal changes in order to become happy.

Positive psychologists support their optimistic positions on human nature and happiness by pointing to recent developments in psychology and other scientific fields, such as neurology and evolution. In the second part of chapter 4 I briefly note some of these other fledgling developments. Then, to round out the array of arguments over happiness, I provide two concrete examples of self-help programs that promise happiness in practice. One, the well-known AA movement, emphasizes the nonsectarian spirituality of its steps to "a new happiness," and the other offers the authority of positive psychology's scientific research for its program. The psychological self-guide is the recently published book by respected researcher Sonja Lyubomirsky, *The How of Happiness: A Scientific Approach to Getting the Life You Want*. Almost too neatly, Dr. Lyubomirsky offers twelve science-based happiness-enhancing exercises that can be compared to AA's spiritually oriented twelve-step program. Unfortunately, I only have room here to look at two practical programs to obtain happiness, although many more paths ranging from Buddhism and beyond await analysis.

Another issue—although we also lack the time and space to address it in detail—is the political and social investigation of the science of happiness. I focus here on the individual's pursuit of happiness, but impressive and large-scale studies are taking place focused on the happiness or subjective well-being of populations and groups. Much of this research includes economic and political variables. Multidisciplinary, multimethod research studies now focus on the comparative happiness of different nations and populations. Such research is useful in the work of policy analysts and government decision makers whose interest lies in increasing a society's general levels of subjective well-being, or gross national happiness (GNH). I confess that when I first heard about GNH several years ago I laughed in surprise. The idea seemed so far out there, perhaps because it was identified with the small, undeveloped Buddhist country of Bhutan. Images of Shangri-la came to mind. But no, quite rapidly this concern for a society's general level of happiness has moved into the cultural mainstream. Serious books, esteemed scholars, and high-level public commissions are appearing. The politics of happiness uses scientific data and research from the new science of happiness. Slowly but surely, policy makers are opening to innovative approaches and policies as various ecological and economic threats increase: global warming, recessions, failing states, and the like. New revolutionary movements for their part may be inspiring other ideas for potential social change. Recently both the Dalai Lama and Pope Benedict XVI have called for the necessary global social changes to achieve happiness and further the common good. For these religious leaders a happy society would be a just society where basic trust and equality of opportunity and dignity exist for each individual.

Certainly the focus of happiness studies on larger populations and institutions provides a background for understanding and generating individual happiness. Humans are a hypersocial species who live with, within, and dependent upon social groups for their well-being. The ways that the larger society operates always influences individuals. But at the same time, individuals influence and construct their social groups. Individuals change the societies they live in as they change themselves, especially perhaps in an affluent, developed society like ours where highly educated individuals enjoy a great deal of autonomy. Americans now are also converting to new faiths in unprecedented numbers. Self-initiative, self-help, and striving for a better life have always been admired in the United States. But when it comes to pursuing happiness in new social psychological ways, skeptics are not hard to find. Resistance to current happiness studies and happiness projects exist.

Skeptics and Resistance

Efforts and movements to find happiness are sometimes brushed off as frivolous and fruitless, a decided waste of intellectual energy, time, and social resources. The pursuit of happiness, say the skeptics, is a Utopian venture, as Thomas Jefferson should have admitted. From ancient times to the present, happiness pessimists have flourished in a number of varieties and flavors. Those who view human life as essentially and inevitably "nasty, brutish and short" can never believe that human happiness is possible. Pessimistic thinkers in every historical period have judged ultimate reality to be meaninglessness and tragic, only to be endured stoically. A realistic goal is to try and reduce the sufferings to which humanity is heir. Happiness pessimists who are atheists refuse any hint of consolation or hope as illusions and deceptions peddled by religion. Intellectual giants of the modern era, such as atheists Sartre and Freud, have asserted the inevitability of human unhappiness as man's fate. For their part, staunch Christian believers of the past, such as Pascal, have also rejected the possibility of human happiness in this fallen and corrupt world. Religious pessimists confine their hope for happiness to the next world, when the faithful have passed through this earthly sinkhole of sin and sorrow.

Brilliant happiness pessimists have been disproportionately influential on modern educated elites in a secular age. Enlightenment optimism and hope for human progress has receded in the wake of the last century's history of war, genocides, torture, atrocities, and private and public abuses of power. Scientific inventions and new technologies have often been used to increase destructiveness.

Pessimists and cynics psychologically disparage experiences of happiness by asserting that they are in reality nothing but relief at the cessation of suffering, always at best temporary. Love, sex, drugs, social games, sport, travel, and other pleasant activities are basically escapes that signify little in the long run. A "happy" person is perceived as permanently self-deceived and innately stupid. For the truly despairing, even the joys of art, creative invention, religion, and altruistic love are fabricated defenses against life's meaninglessness and misery. Illusions of happiness are lies, albeit vital lies, serving only to create false hopes. Only children and the childish can cling to the magical belief that human happiness exists— somewhere over the rainbow where bluebirds sing. Actually "never-never land" is more like it. Adults must face the fact that from birth to death humans who manage to survive infancy endure pain, frustration, fear, anxiety, grief, and progressive deterioration until death.

Great poets and literary geniuses, like persuasive philosophers, also give voice to melancholy and despair. Few more moving and beautiful laments can be found than Matthew Arnold's "Dover Beach." In an address to his beloved, Arnold writes that the world which looks "So various, so beautiful, so new, / Hath really neither joy, nor love, nor light, / Nor certitude, nor peace, nor help for pain. / And we are here as on a darkling plain / Swept with confused alarms of struggle and flight, / Where ignorant armies clash by night."

For Arnold, religion can provide no hope since the sea of religious faith has long receded from the world's shores and neither science nor religion can provide certitude. Pain and delusion reign. At least in Arnold's case, lovers still can be true to one another. Other skeptics would dismiss even that consolation. While sex, physical pleasure, and ego satisfactions can briefly stimulate individuals, these moments do not last. Why not? Because humans quickly lose the positive feelings of reward as they adapt or habituate to them. As each positive stimulus loses its effect, new ones are sought. Dissatisfaction and frustration are man's lot, as he is trapped by nature on a hedonic treadmill of escalating desires.

The endless process of pursuing future rewards is judged by one happiness researcher to be built into human nature by evolutionary processes; they serve to ensure survival. Happiness is the bait, lure, or ruse that keeps humans struggling toward reproducing generation after generation. People cannot change themselves or the cycle. The merry-go-round continues to spin, leaving individuals to their sentimental and self-deceiving illusions of happiness.

Other resisters of the current happiness boom are not so despairing or pessimistic. They may simply dismiss the self-help industry promising happiness as the latest fad or junk science to exploit the gullible. Enough evidence is available to validate the skeptics. The popular media hypes any and all research findings no matter their quality and blithely jumbles together all those proposing the pursuit of happiness. Professionally trained scientific researchers are lumped in with any instant gurus who gain a following. America is wired for access to new information; all therapeutic claims become immediately and widely publicized on *Oprah* or the Web.

Self-help programs of all kinds are everywhere and constitute a highly profitable industry. There are happiness fairs, conferences, and Web sites where suspect and substantive offerings appear side by side. Different wares are for sale, but signing up for a series of expensive sessions that guarantee happiness in three months does not seem a good bet. If a happiness expert is an untrained entrepreneur, all the more reason to flee. Spending good money investing in a "happiness makeover" may not be a wise move. Caveat emptor.

My local paper recently featured an amusing example of America's mixed-up happiness scene. The front-page story in a popular new Mind & Body section began with the authoritative statement, "Researchers including professors Daniel Gilbert of Harvard University and Sonja Lyubomirsky of the University of California are finding that the road to happiness is paved with more than fluffy pop-psychology mumbo jumbo. There is a real science behind human happiness, and there are concrete tools proven to make life more satisfying." This opening salvo was followed by the comment that "in the current economy, happiness is hot."

The story continued, giving most of the space to interviewing a local media star who bills herself as a "mind-set coach"; she is a devotee of the gospel of positive thinking, guaranteed to lead to happiness. Every personal tragedy should be viewed as an opportunity to become happier. Confidently, the coach or guru provides her instant positive directions for finding happiness. On her popular television program she advertises the sale of her happiness advisory services. As authority and validation of her advice she invokes reliance on her intuition. In addition to her public media stints she has private clients, and she markets tapes and books. She also sells bottled water.

The news story seamlessly continued to describe the work of the highly credentialed scientific researcher, professor Sonja Lyubomirsky, who in addition to her renowned academic and teaching roles, markets her popular self-help book (*The How of Happiness*, discussed in chapter 6). Lyubomirsky also runs an iPhone "Live Happy Program." One of academic psychology's goals as a helping profession is to give psychology away. Yet as professionals, psychologists also see themselves entitled to charge fees for service. Lyubomirsky claims that her work is scientifically sound and a self-help program that actually works to help people. Unfortunately, the media's indiscriminate coverage of whatever is "hot" in happiness studies can end up including a lot of "fluffy pop-psychology mumbo jumbo." Critics can't be blamed if they end up dismissing happiness studies along with astrology.

Moral and Aesthetic Resistance

Another kind of resistance to the pursuit-of-happiness movement is not so much a reservation over its scientific validity but consists of moral and aesthetic concerns. Diverting energy and social resources away from needed efforts to remedy the world's suffering can seem unjustifiable. But this argument is countered by noting that happy people are found to be more willing and able to dedicate themselves to altruistic actions on behalf of relieving suffering. More happiness can lead to more resources for helping others. Happiness in moral critiques is often misidentified as selfish hedonism.

Another beneficial characteristic of happiness and subjective well-being is that happiness can help prevent an individual's or group's descent into languishing or wasted lives, leading to depression. Happy people are shown to be healthier; to live longer; to be more socially engaged, more altruistic, optimistic, and energized for new ventures; and to be more creative in problem solving. The benefits springing from subjective well-being are many. When things go badly happiness also helps people overcome the disasters and be more resilient.

It can be morally argued that if happiness is a good and socially positive benefit, denying its pursuit to the many who can benefit because not everyone can yet be helped would be wrong. Even if many existing evils and misfortunes exist, it would seem wrong to deny potential goods for others who can receive them. Certainly, fortunate persons in a society have moral obligations to relieve the poverty and suffering of those for whom they reasonably can, but they are not obligated to spurn the benefits of happiness for themselves or their children—especially if becoming happy helps people cope when bad things happen to good people.

I suspect, moreover, that some resistance to happiness studies is not so much moral but often is a case of aesthetic or culturally conditioned distaste. Implicit norms of culture and class affect lifestyles and attitudes. An old-school English matron could refuse to participate in a local happiness research project with the words, "Sorry, we're English. We don't do happiness here." Or as the author Tony Judt, heroically dying from Lou Gehrig's disease, replied when refusing to lecture on his struggles, "I was raised in Britain and we don't do uplift."

Do elites and heroes pursue happiness, or do they work at mastering a stoic indifference to fate? Courageous self-mastery can actually bring a form of proud and self-contented happiness, but it is not always understood in this way. An individual can learn at his tutor's knee that indifference to emotions or *apatheia* is the highest achievement of virtuous character. Better to fall on your sword than plead for an ignoble reprieve. Certain cultural circles can look down their noses at self-help endeavors, including happiness. Isn't it a confession of either weakness or ill breeding to be centered on your own subjective emotional wellbeing? Only the crude and crass call attention to their needs or deeds.

Psychological movements like the "triumph of the therapeutic" in post–World War II American society have been excoriated as a sign of cultural decay, seen as thinly disguised self-worship in the guise of psychotherapy's search for happiness. Rather, in a good society, individuals and groups should be striving for the common good, unselfishly and unselfconsciously. They will ask what they can do for their country and other people, not take their own emotional temperature to gauge their happiness. The lament is heard that, with the rise of modern expressive individualism, psychology and therapy substitute for morality and religion. Decline and fall await, and so on and so on.

I no longer am in sympathy with the above views and have moved on from my origins in a cultural mind-set that disdained psychology and the pursuit of subjective happiness. I am not British or Irish, but was raised in a southern military family with agrarian colonial roots. We were all firmly Protestant and Calvinist in tradition. The religious belief and practice had mellowed somewhat over the generations, but not the moral values inherited. Dedicated to patriotic West Point ideals of honor, duty, and country, we disdained self-assertion, self-analysis, or selfish materialism as crude and rude, or damn-Yankee traits. This code—part populist, part cavalier—demanded uprightness, good manners, honor, and duty rather than subjective happiness. Keep your word, and fulfill your obligations. Never complain, never whine, and when suffering comes, buck up and suck it up. Psychological therapy equaled weakness of character. Who are you to demand that the universe cater to your desires? Work harder; duty trumps your druthers.

Fortunately, the outcome of generations of southern piety provided an unnoticed positive character to the culture. While not consciously stressed, the moral and religious virtues inculcated produced happiness. Altruistic neighborly giving and nurturing sociability were cultural norms. Traditions of conviviality, hospitality, storytelling, wit, playfulness, and merry high spirits (including alcohol for males) generated happiness. Communities close to nature with a slower pace induced happiness along with mutual help. Thus, paradoxically, the culture produced the habits of happiness without giving much mind or respect for its pursuit. Intellectuals and academics could be less admired because they were prone to overthinking everything and were self-involved. The takeaway message I received was clear: don't be too smart or too religious to fit in, and become a charming, positive person, upright, happy, and helpful to all—without consciously trying.

It was also the norm, if not mandatory, for women to be strong, to marry, and to vigorously take care of their kinfolk—although my marrying a philosopher and having six children was thought to be eccentric. I also became the subject of suspicion when my individual journey led to intense religious interests (becoming a Roman Catholic, no less!), combined with equally intense intellectual pursuits. I doggedly pursued a PhD in psychology along with a writing career. This lifelong intellectual effort to synthesize theological and psychological knowledge with family life has given me (full disclosure) a wonderfully happy life.

Slowly, it appears in hindsight, I have worked my way toward the subject of happiness. By now I have written many books and articles on women, family, sexuality, conscience, and most recently a book on the relationship of joy and suffering in Christianity. Obviously I have long since passed beyond all intellectual or aesthetic resistance to psychology and happiness studies.

My purpose in this book is to explore but also argue for certain optimistic positions. I see the increasing scientific, intellectual, and spiritual study of happiness as progress, a very good thing, made better by successful practical applications. My advocacy, however, does not blind me to the value of critiquing positions and cultivating doubt and different sources of insight. I draw on theological, literary, humanistic, and scientific knowledge. How grateful I am for the work of the multitude of scholars, scientists, and theological thinkers who have informed and formed me.

My intellectual commitments and values do not, I trust, keep me from giving a full hearing to the arguments of those whose views differ from mine. "I seek to be among the less deceived" is a good mantra for intellectuals and religious believers who know how fallible they are. Doubt and a critical eye are always necessary, but a critical eye need not be a cold eye, nor preclude taking positions.

Clearly I am also endorsing a very optimistic view of the potential of theology, psychology, and science to help humans change their views and themselves. But I contend that this stance is neither unrealistic or illusory. I am also a convinced Christian believer, and so I argue that religious and spiritual wisdom can bring happiness or blessedness in this life as well as the next. At every Roman Catholic Mass, the celebrating priest proclaims, "Happy are those who are called to your table." The liturgy overflows with scriptural commands to rejoice and be glad.

Yet in a secular age, religious good news and other positive signs of the time can be easily discounted. The bad news always seems so much more real than the glad tidings. Evolution may have predisposed us to pay more attention to pain, danger, and vivid negative emotional signals so that we take instant defensive actions in order to survive. By contrast, the delight of happiness and the exuberance of joy can appear far less serious or grave. Perhaps giving up gravitas is a first step in getting to the truth of happiness. The initial question dances ahead: What is the definition of happiness?

Chapter 2

WHAT IS HAPPINESS?

Children love to sing the old song, "If you're happy and you know it, clap your hands." In the many verses that follow, you must tap your toe and move other body parts to show that you know you're happy. The fact that children can be so sure that they recognize happiness when they see it or feel it might suggest that defining happiness is a simple matter. But no, things get complicated right away. In fact, arguments over the definition of happiness have been going on for millennia, at least from the time of Aristotle and the ancient Greek philosophers. During the meetings of our recent Pursuit of Happiness Project, some of the most heated disagreements were over the definition of happiness.

What, for instance, is going to count as happiness, and whose point of view should be given the final say? If you think you are happy and everybody else in society thinks you're crazy or deluded, whose judgment should prevail? When a clinical diagnosis of mania is determined, you can be hospitalized. Then again, in sane individuals, how much happy time is required to be counted as happy? Does a surge of joy once in a blue moon prove the possession of happiness? Some theorists would say either a preponderance, or a three-to-one ratio, of positive to negative emotions is required for you and your days to count as happy and bright. Some gloomier observers say that one should only be called happy after death—when presumably no further disasters, like rotten adult children or other guilty shames, can overtake you. In a culture that seeks to minimize family status and reputation, only your own individual integrity can

15

determine your state of mind. And you don't have to wait for death to make the call. Isn't happiness an inner individual experience to which only you have the access code?

In these disputes I'm on the side of those who define happiness as an inner emotional experience of a conscious and sane human being. It is I who am happy, I who feel the positive emotions that I'm saying yes to, and want to continue; let it be, let it be. Happiness feels good in every bone of my body and mind. No amount of philosophical disdain for "smiley-faced emotions" or comments about "the triviality of pleasure" can dissuade happy people from knowing that they live as bodies who are happy when they experience positive pleasures and good feelings. The yes of happiness energizes, enlivens, and makes us feel whole and together. I know it's happiness when it lifts and lightens the heart, buoys the mind, and energizes the body. In happiness, people actively engage and relate with, through, and in the other—be it another person, myself, a group, God, or my puppy Sunshine. Happiness is lot more than a warm puppy, but I recognize the basic emotion being described.

Happiness is also relating rightly to myself as a whole and feeling congruent or together. The philosophers are therefore right when they say happiness includes the kind of good feeling I get when my life is going well. When what I am emotionally happy about seems okay and morally acceptable since it does no harm to myself or others, then it can count as positive, unalloyed happiness. Realizing that one's life in general is filled with happy emotional experiences that are meaningful and worthwhile is often named "authentic," "real," "true," "lasting," or "flourishing" happiness. In defining happiness we have the long and the short of it, the inside and the outside views, as well as the positive emotion and the positive valuation.

One working definition that brings these good strands together comes from Sonja Lyubomirsky, the positive psychologist, whom we met in the last chapter and will meet again in chapter 6. In her how-to-be-happy self-help book, she defines happiness as "the experience of joy, contentment or positive well-being, combined with a sense that one's life is good, meaningful and worthwhile." Happiness is present when my positive good feelings are embedded within a life that seems valuable. This robust definition of happiness covers a lot of territory and allows for being happy during difficult hard times if they are part of a meaningful life.

But what about a baby or a mentally impaired person who doesn't have the cognitive equipment to judge life as worthwhile or meaningful? Are they incapable of happiness? As I kept insisting in our group arguments, "There's something wrong with your definition of happiness if it excludes babies." Granted, babies live in the moment and don't have language to help them think about abstract concepts. But Sonja L's definition of happiness can still work for babies since she is careful to refer to "a sense" of a worthwhile life. To sense something, or to intuit or feel it, doesn't require articulated words or abstract rational categories of thought. It is more basic and immediate. A happy baby or an Alzheimer's patient who does not or no longer possesses the linguistic capacity to explicitly define values can have a positive sense of joy, goodness, and happiness. As it turns out, a huge amount of adult information processing also takes place nonconsciously without explicit self-awareness. What we used to call intuition or sensing, we now call the adapted nonconscious (more on this in chapter 4).

A more troublesome question to mull over is the one about whose meanings or values are going to define happiness, especially if there are conflicting views. Here a personal memory comes to mind of a family difference over happiness that took place many decades ago. One cold winter during our poverty-stricken graduate school days, my father, a nonreligious retired navy captain, came to visit. He had heard that we were enthusiastic followers of Dorothy Day's *Catholic Worker* and believed all that odd stuff about God, poverty, and providence. But when he got a good look at our spartan life of 24/7 hard physical and intellectual labor, with three babies under three living in a shabby slum apartment, he became upset.

"But Sidney, Sidney," he kept saying. "You really can't be happy living like this."

But yes, in fact, I really was happy. The external hardships seemed but a bracing challenge, a backdrop to the loving, joyful fulfillment of bearing and caring for babies. We were fighting the good fight for God and survival. And also flourishing, since this was poverty in Harvard Square bursting with intellectual stimulation as well as support from a band of Catholic academics. I felt like a warrior queen on crusade or at least an enthusiastic pilgrim in Jerusalem. Wordsworth's lines on his early Paris adventure during the French Revolution applied to me: "Bliss was it in that dawn to be alive, / But to be young was very heaven!" Of course, a blissful student crusade tends to mellow into middle-class family life, but the happiness of a well-spent youth can never be taken from you. I don't think I ever convinced my worried worldly father, but he promptly sent me a washing machine and dryer, definitely boosting my material happiness as a diaper-impailed young mother.

In a more serious problem of conflicting definitions of happiness, philosophers are wont to bring up the case of the happy Nazi soldier who is a normal, ordinary individual. Like the majority of the German Army he cannot be classified as a psychopath, psychotic, or serial killer in a uniform. Psychopaths, psychotics, and serial killers may sometimes speak of being happy, but their impaired emotional and cognitive makeup casts doubt on their self-assessments. But Nazis who were completely sane could claim to be happy and see themselves leading meaningful and worthwhile lives congruent with their beliefs. Such cases are sobering because they witness to the historical fact that persons can be formed and socialized into moral worlds that are now viewed as morally abhorrent. When family, tribe, religion, and leaders have all agreed on the definition of the good and happy life, could an individual know any better than to conform? If individuals have no way of knowing any better, they can hardly be held responsible for their attitudes and actions. The innocently ignorant who claim happiness can be understood in retrospect. I can understand the happy Nazi because, as a child of an American military family, I remember the resounding joy when we dropped the atomic bomb on a Japanese city and wiped out so many of our enemies. Definitions of meaningful happiness can change as moral understandings of truth change.

The many disputes encountered in defining happiness have produced some rueful reactions among scholars confronting the new interest in happiness studies. The philosopher Nicholas White concludes, in his brief history of happiness in Western thought, that it might be better to give up trying to define happiness since we may be searching "for something that's unobtainable." Better to use different words to describe the different kinds of states now too generally labeled "happiness."

Other investigators working in the new science of happiness counter with more optimistic solutions to the definition problem. Researcher Daniel Nettle, for one, recognizes the difficulties of defining what happiness is, but claims that there is surely *something* that people mean by the word. Doesn't everyone outside of certain philosophers give evidence that they understand what is meant? Nettle's proposal for resolving the definition problem is to claim that there is a continuum of different levels and kinds of happiness, such as Levels 1, 2, and 3. A core primary reality of happiness can be granted as basic, but capable of being expanded and extended as more and more meanings are added into the mix. An intuitive core experience of emotional happiness, joy, and valued pleasure constitutes Level 1, and also can be broadened and elaborated at other, more complicated levels. To my mind this makes good sense and is true to my experience. Yes, let's acknowledge that a common core of good-good emotional-evaluative experience is what we essentially mean by happiness, but accept that many further elaborated varieties and flavors can be included. The continuum of happiness can range from ecstatic moments to prolonged contentment and satisfaction. With more evaluative thoughtfulness and stability, the more a moral and social perspective becomes salient. Remember that interpersonal relationships, real and imagined, always play a powerful role in hypersocial human beings. I am never wandering lonely as a cloud through life, but always subject to surrounding wind, temperature, and prevailing atmospheric conditions. Unspoken and voiced conversations of self and others are playing within my stream of consciousness and inducing responses that include emotions. An individual is formed by and constantly lives within the ongoing social matrix. So we understand the happy Nazi and our own American forebears as well.

In every cultural group the family socializes a child into the group's moral norms and customs. They, the neighbors, and the nation provide the words, definitions, cultural norms, comparisons, and framing beliefs that affect our emotional happiness. Yet there are innately evolved universal patterns of emotions that underlie the shaping. Happiness is a human universal and universally recognized. Naturally the others in the immediate social group provide the words, definitions, cultural norms, comparisons, and framing beliefs that affect our emotional happiness. But positive emotions of joy, interest, and love are also basic, evolved, innate responses that underlie social shaping. Happiness exists as a real something that can be known and also comes in different variations. Many complex realities and concepts like happiness are recognized as real but defy narrow definitions and boundaries. The term "fuzzy logic" has been coined for the way certain real things cannot be confined or precisely delimited. "Happiness" may be like the idea of a "game," or a "family" in which a reality can be recognized as taking a variety of forms. Every "family" is not identical to every other family; every "game" is not constituted by the same rules, yet we understand what is meant. So, too, real experiences of happiness can range on a continuum and on levels, with different degrees of intensity, breadth, mixtures, and shifting patterns.

Have we not all felt an ecstatic joy that subsides into calm gladness, or a serene contented satisfaction that flares up into exhilaration? A deft image to describe the different patterns of positive emotion is found in a short story by J. D. Salinger. The hero of the adventure finds employment in a fly-by-night writing school; he has some exciting successes in his work before eventually quitting. Commenting on what he has learned he says, "The most singular difference between happiness and joy is that happiness is a solid and joy a liquid." When his joy "leaked out," he departed. Yes, water appears in different forms, and so does happiness. Fountains, rivers, mists, snow, and ice are one and the same, yet different. Fire is also a compelling image for depicting the burning and different kinds of happiness—from a soaring bonfire to banked glowing embers warming the hearth.

Unsurprisingly, dramatic bonfires have garnered a great deal of fascinated attention on the happiness continuum. Vivid, surging flames of intense joy and delight can appear instantly out of nowhere. Psychologists have labeled these moments "peak experiences" or "epiphanies." They appear as heightened moments of consciousness and have been described in religious writing as well as literary fiction. Intense peak experiences of joyful happiness appear infused with a radiance that brings a felt assurance that blessedness and goodness unite the whole universe. Yes, yes, all will be well, all will be well, all will be exceedingly well. The rising up of joy transcends and transforms the routines and landscapes of mundane existence.

With less intensity, eruptions of laughter, play, wit, and humor also lift and heighten energy; be merry, gentlepersons, let nothing us dismay. Playful happiness as well as deeply calm happiness extends and energizes the horizons of life. Whether in low comedy or high wit, humor breaks out of the predictable expectation and surprises us. Moments of joy and happiness are mysterious in their origin.

Poets have claimed that heightened moments of happy inspiration arrive from the Muses, or bubble up from the depths of nature and the creative riches of earth's own wonderful life. Religious mystics and believers attribute such joyful tongues of fire to the descent and infusion of God's Divine Spirit. When we turn next to consider God and happiness, we find understanding of God as the Divine Liveliness pouring forth life, love, joy, novelty, and truth as Divine gifts ancient and ever new. God is known as generating the joyful energy of the universe from within; God is Happiness and so is encountered as a loving and playful Creator. In a believing Christian's perspective, joy and gladness emerge as an unveiling of ultimate truth; the world is charged with the glory of God. As I argue in the next chapter, happiness can be received as a message or call from God. Throughout the creation, happiness evidences God's good existence and the Divine invitation to unity and transformation. The definition of happiness in Christian faith incorporates and comprehensively frames human definitions and experiences. To become happy you seek union with God, who seeks union with you.

And here, before moving on to more religious reflections or examining the science of happiness with its "how to become happy" interventions, it is worth noting that epiphanies and joyful peak experiences, or even bursts of play, humor, and laughter, arrive spontaneously and involuntarily, not as artifacts constructed from conscious efforts of will. Religious believers view these experiences as unearned gifts of grace. Science will have to do its own explanatory turn, perhaps trying to see how evolution and natural forces can be the deep wellsprings of humanity's positive emotions.

In efforts to increase happiness, the most effective strategy may lie in making efforts to prepare the readiness to receive what nature (or the Divine Spirit) brings. We climb the hill at dawn to enjoy the glorious sunrise but don't manufacture it to order, nor have we earned it by right. Many a man, woman, and child has been "surprised by joy" as an unearned gift. When psychological researchers try to invoke positive emotions in the lab, they use natural symbols of beauty and mood-inducing music or comic movies or actors instructed to induce contagious good cheer. If they resort to drugs or drink, they are not studying naturally occurring happiness anymore. In the happiness sweepstakes, not only ripeness but readiness is all.

Fortunately, in a beautiful, wonder-filled world, nature, spirituality, love, and art are generously abundant and contribute to readiness. Art, particularly literature, can be a rich and most reliable resource for inducing happiness; art using words and verbal meanings can generate happiness and simultaneously communicate understandings of the experience. The language of empirical science with its definitions and descriptions is plain and flat. Experimenters seek the plainest, most straightforward, and least ambiguous words to ensure that everyone understands everything in the same way. When replication is a necessary standard for reliability and validity, words must be crystal clear. And better that mathematics could be used to measure and quantify the object of inquiry. But happiness is not a material object; rather it is an inner conscious experience. And human consciousness is still the ultimate unknown frontier of the human intellectual quest. No one yet understands how it relates to a physical entity like the brain, or how it works. When we realize that happiness is an experience of consciousness, then it becomes part of the unknown. Even more challenging is the effort to direct consciousness by human efforts, as in intentionally becoming happy. Measuring the empirical effects of happiness on individuals and groups may be a less daunting task, but effectively increasing happiness in a human group may bring us back to the big problem. In pursuing the full understandings of happiness we can see that thousands more books need to be written, and will be welcome. Science is a great ally in the quest, along with other treasure troves of human wisdom. So naturally, the others in the immediate social group provide the words, definitions, cultural norms, comparisons, and framing beliefs that affect our emotional happiness, found in the arts, religion, and literature.

Art and literature have one great advantage in conveying wisdom: they give delight and so can generate happiness as they portray it. The medium is the message whether hot or cool. Insights into happiness emerge in poetry, drama, music, dance, painting, and rituals of different kinds that combine all of the above with words and the Word. The repetitive litany of experiences that bring happiness include love, work, play, sex, childbirth, sensual pleasures, rescue from danger, immersion in nature, family, friendship, worship, and intellectual problem solving and discovery.

The rich quality of emotions and the dynamic, multileveled varieties of ongoing human consciousness often have been compared to music. Musical chords, melodies, and fugues containing different themes and color, tempo, and patterns emerge, soar, fall away, and reappear in new combinations. The reverberation, resonance, and nuance of music govern our responses and provide the similarities to our qualitative streams of conscious happiness. The ever-moving quicksilver quality of consciousness and emotion is one major reason happiness is so hard to pin down and define with words.

However, one literary art form—the modern novel—has been singled out as particularly effective in its ability to convey the flow of inner subjective conscious experience and to produce understanding of it. In a novel the words and narrative, without music or moving images, convey rich emotional experience. An internal, first-person point of view can be interwoven with description from an external, objective, third-person perspective on events. Dialogues can also be inserted that contribute to the ongoing plot, revelations of character, and the emotional tone. The narrative gives the reader a framework in which the imagined characters' emotional responses and thoughts emerge as meaningful. Hearing the inner voice of characters and accounts of ongoing events ingeniously creates vicarious emotional experiences for the reader. We also would feel this way in this or that situation. Readers project with empathy into the world created by words; and they can be transported out of self into the reality constructed by the author. A novel, like music, can capture our attention and direct consciousness while drawing forth our emotions. Sophisticated literary critical theories have analyzed these techniques for evoking emotional consciousness. But even when ignorant of the analyses, the power and insights of a novel and story can be felt. No wonder novels were thought to be dangerous for the young to read. It is also easy to understand why all known human cultures have included storytelling as an activity that informs, instructs, celebrates, and conveys accounts of living that give delight.

Characters in novels can be shown undergoing inner experiences of happiness in all of its various levels, degrees, nuances, resonances, and configurations. Then, through the use of flexible prose techniques, the person can be portrayed as reacting to and reflecting upon their own thoughts and emotional feelings. Their emotional impressions, as in real life, reveal more of themselves to the reader, and while narrators can be unreliable, they are attended to with interest and suspense. Inevitably the pursuit and experience of happiness are center stage in their concerns. Two examples of acclaimed British novels are illuminating.

In his highly praised 2007 novel *Oxygen*, Andrew Miller creates a character who experiences intense happiness, and then reflects upon it. Lazlo, an Eastern European playwright, muses to himself on the morning after a joy-filled reunion with old comrades from the Hungarian revolution. "Happiness," he thinks, "was a subject as elusive as love, and one that required a similar subtlety of lexis and category. . . . There was public happiness, such as the day of the football match, joy reflected back from the faces of everyone he saw. And secret happiness, as when he was in love with Peter, almost a burden, as though he had won the lottery yet could share the news with no one. Pure happiness was rare, confined in most cases to infants, drug fiends and religious ecstatics."

Lazlo goes on to wonder (as do psychologists) about the strange way that different kinds of happiness can coexist with other emotions, even with terror, as in the joy he felt in the street battles against Russian tanks. He compares his emotional experiences to music, poetry, and spirituality. Happiness has given him a sudden sense of "well-being that overwhelmed me . . . as if I had been seized by the present and shaken out, or had sensed—forgive me—my own immortal soul, something I find hard to believe in most days of the week." Lazlo, like James Joyce and others before him, calls the sudden surge of radiant happiness and insight "a little epiphany." As a character who is a writer by vocation, Lazlo is inspired to recite the poet Rilke's lines, "And we who always think of happiness *rising* would feel the emotion that almost startles us when a happy thing *falls*." Rilke's lines reveal that poets share the powers of evoking emotions through words. The novel can include a poem but not the other way around.

Andrew Miller's prose creates a world in which a reader can gain insight into the elusive nature of happiness. The experience is shown as private and personal as well as collective and public. Happiness is received like a gift that increases well-being and spiritual insight. In streams of conscious emotions, happiness can become associated with other thoughts and emotions but is still distinct.

In an equally fascinating British novel, even more focused on the pursuit of happiness, Michael Frayn's *Landing on the Sun* defines the search for happiness as central to the plot. In this dark comedy two senior academics are assigned to write a government white paper on the topic of happiness (and this fiction preceded the popular concern with gross national happiness movements). The high-level foreign office bureaucrat, Summerfield, is assigned to work with a learned woman philosopher to produce the report. The Oxford philosopher is an unhappily married woman, and Summerfield is a dutifully married family man who loves his daughter. His recognition of how his love for his daughter makes him happy is a discovery, along with the fact that he doesn't love his wife. As the two dutiful researchers proceed in their project they become more and more personally attracted to one another; without meaning to, they fall deeply in love. As their love increases in intensity they become ecstatically happy in their union of mind and heart and the companionable working time spent together in an out-of-the-way government office. They make surprising discoveries about their subject. One is that they can know with certainly that, yes, they are happy in being together. Their dictated report, later found in the file, becomes less and less academic and more personally revealing. Before the final disaster occurs and the tape abruptly ends, a final recorded exchange has Summerfield suddenly presenting a definition of happiness: "I should say that happiness is being where one is and not wanting to be anywhere else."

"Yes, I think you're right," his colleague and lover replies. "Thank you."

The novel is a comic masterpiece that delights the reader as it simultaneously conveys what an experience of happiness actually is, against the background of all that has been said about it in intellectual discourse. The verbal and the nonverbal senses of happiness are played out against each other, as the problem of definition is wrestled with. Both are powerful in revealing and understanding the perennially magnetic appeal of happiness in human life.

Words are incomparable in re-creating human experiences and understanding them. The countless artistic expressions of happiness can provide their messages and meanings by engaging the five senses as well as linguistic re-creations of thought and feeling. The recent claims that music, dance, and art were as important as language in the evolution of Homo sapiens are worth remembering. Evidence has been gathered in prehistoric cave paintings, artifacts, and burial mounds of the importance of visual art and musical celebration—and by implication expressions of happiness. Even today dancing in groups, whether in the streets or not, expresses communal joy and happiness; it serves to heighten gladness. Engaging in valued relationships that transcend the boundaries of self brings happiness. It is good to be where one is and with these others here and now.

And more fortunately, in big-brained humans the capacity to enjoy now is augmented by the ability to remember past joys and imagine a bright future. By savoring the present, happiness is expanded and enhanced by time past and time future. Gratefully contrasting present good feelings with past negative ones can also be a factor in increasing happiness. And perhaps most significantly, human brain power also includes capacities for empathy and identification with others, doubling and tripling present delights through sharing joyful consciousness. Emotions are contagious, and joyful happiness spreads and increases as it resonates with the joy of others—sometimes down through history, as both followers of Buddha and Christ would claim.

Underlying the truism that love and work make up a good and happy life is the fact that both love and work involve the self's engagement in valued relationships beyond self. Whether as a nursing baby, a nursing mother, or a philosopher king, a self's affirmative yes to the relationship with the other—God, lover, baby, friend, or group—brings the good and valued high of happiness. Let it be, let it be, let the good times roll and never end. The enjoyment and overflowing reverberations of happiness generate gratitude—which works to increase happiness. Or as G. K. Chesterton characteristically commented, "Gratitude is happiness doubled by wonder." Conversely, happiness is tripled by gratitude; happiness in all its degrees expands, enlarges, enhances, enlivens, stimulates, delights, integrates, focuses, and integrates human beings.

In all of the interrelated understandings and definitions, evolutionary psychologists would see happiness and positive relating processes as made possible by the innately evolved positive emotions of joy, love, and interest. But at times the happiness arising from interest and discovery is given less attention than love and joy. It should not be forgotten that the positive emotion of interest gives happiness from engaging with realities that are not interpersonal or social. Persons can be happy when in solitude they are engaged in discovery, invention, problem solving, creating art, or working. The aha experience of problem solving is a moment of joy; the creation of an artwork or work project gives gladness. Being engrossed in any task or activity in the world can give happiness. Children become rapt in their play, called their "love affair with the world," and adults can love their work.

Individuals can be made happy when carried away by an intense interest in a task or activity that is neither too difficult nor too easy. Recent studies of optimal experiences call these absorbing conscious states "flow." The effort of give-and-take in pursuing the activity requires focused attention and recursive decision making. As the self is attending and concentrating on the process, the person becomes absorbed and a kind of self-forgetfulness sets in. Time and the outside environment fade away or recede. People forget themselves or lose track of time. Who has not been intensely absorbed in talking, in work, in sex, in playing or watching a game, in a movie, or in reading? In religious life, mystics and ordinary worshipers become caught up in liturgical rituals and prayer. The basic positive emotion of interest can become conjoined with love and joy. Paradoxically such self-forgetful absorptions end up enhancing and enlarging the self that is given over to the active task. Star athletes speak of "being in the zone" or being "hot," and great dancers claim that "the dancer becomes the dance." A self can consciously begin, initiate, and direct an activity but then become absorbed.

After episodes of flow, or even coming up for air in the process, persons can again become explicitly aware of themselves and know that they are happy. The interesting thing is that they are not conscious of being happy while they are absorbed. This must explain why persons sometimes report that they didn't know they were happy, back when they were in the midst of some episode, but only realized it later. Also they may not have been directly seeking happiness at the time but instead were intensely interested in some task; then happiness, like love is said to do, walked in. All kinds of good consequences appear to come to those who experience the happiness of flow states. Perhaps these positive effects arise from an individual's capacities to focus attention on an activity in the here and now. The processing of flow—the focusing of attention, the perseverance of effort, the ability of appropriately gauging the effort needed—appear as constituents of happiness. An everyday definition of happiness that emphasizes its quality of interested activity comes from an Iris Murdoch character in another British novel. Iris Murdoch, a novelist and a prominent Oxford philosopher, has a character in one of her novels say, "Happiness is a matter of one's most everyday mode of consciousness being busy and lively and unconcerned with self." This is a domesticated, undramatic definition of happiness that may characterize the lives of the multitudes of people who report to happiness researchers that they are "moderately" or "very happy."

The more ecstatic end of the continuum of happiness feelings may be expressed by shouting, singing, laughing, dancing, leaping, or tears of joy, perhaps even swooning or "dying" of happiness (as with those Pentecostals who are slain in the Spirit?). On the other hand, in secret happiness a person can inwardly exult in silence and be outwardly calm. My felt joy may be only disclosed by subtle and fleeting micro expressions of the face—as can be evidenced on videos and film—or by images of physiological or brain arousal. As a socialized member of my family group, my happiness will include internalized emotional display rules as well as standards of value and meaning. I can be happy by behaving well according to my considered values—especially under provocation. The words, "Well done, good and faithful servant," produce intense happiness. The more serene, thought-filled forms of happiness may be more under my control and endure longer. Peak experiences and ecstatic moments arrive unpredictably and can be too physically wearing to sustain. Serene happiness can last.

Fortunately, serene happiness has not been ignored in artistic creations. A quiet, contained happiness, for instance, appears to be a special characteristic of Vermeer's paintings or a Mozart symphony. Perhaps even an architectural building like the Parthenon could be a happiness-generating work of art. Calm gladness can also be described by verbal means in poetry and prose. I can be content "like a weaned child on its mother's breast," or my beloved and I can walk on the shore and know that "the sea is bright and calm tonight."

A delighted contemplative receptivity is one moment in the fulsome story of the continuum of happiness. Equanimity and peace evoke another kind of deeper, calmer kind of happiness. A puzzling challenge for understanding happiness arises when persons claim that they are intensely happy while undergoing dreadful experiences in awful circumstances. Individuals have reported themselves to be happy and joyful while incarcerated in the gulag, or suffering from debilitating and painful diseases, or while being persecuted and tortured as missionaries or reformers. In the most extreme cases, martyrs have gone singing to their deaths, displaying joy in the midst of pain and distress. Indian warriors have engaged in triumphant death songs while being flayed alive. In less violent instances, stoic philosophers, saints, and sages have serenely accepted their unjust imprisonment and executions. How so?

Here again answers may lie in the fact that a highly developed human consciousness can operate at different levels of self-awareness and in parallel structures. Persons can acquire different levels of consciousness and identity and direct their emotional responses by freely deploying and sustaining attention as they will. Some imagery that has been used to describe these levels and operations of personal conscious control include innermost or more central core identities of a self that become so strong, enduring, and powerful that they can determine more peripheral stimuli from outside. Some centered, core, valued dimensions of a person have been described as "hot" because they are so emotionally invested in and owned, in contrast to cooler, less valued, transitory responses. But the point to be made in the happiness question is that mature and developed persons can possess deep, central, enduring, emotionally invested core operating identities that engender sustained happiness, even in the midst of ongoing negative stimuli and painful perceptions. Some deep, highly valued, owned dimensions of a self's relationships may persist and be more powerful in determining happiness than surface reactions and hardships. The owned and foundational character of a person can exert more power over his or her experience of happiness than the sufferings being endured. Happiness emerges from the possession of deeper, more potent personal resources than the powers of inflicted pain. Such heroic character strength may be rare, or perhaps more common than we know. In any case, inspiring exemplars have encouraged their fellows throughout history and provide us with new questions about becoming happy.

Is it true that "Iron bars do not a prison make"? Survival stories of Vietnam prisons, concentration camps, gulags, or other grim, abusive hells give glimpses of how much travail and abuse human beings can overcome with moments of happiness still present. The sources of happiness can be past memories, bonds with fellow sufferers, and glimpses of the natural world—the spider web, the mouse, the sun or moon, or flower in the cranny wall. Human consciousness in rare spirits cannot easily be broken. Memory and hope can actively counter present misery; remembered love brings happiness. Acts of empathic love and altruism serve as another strong shield against despair. The key human capacity is the ability to direct and sustain attention to the good and have consciousness follow. Extreme conditions of life with its heroic examples give hope that everyday people like ourselves can become happy.

Some cultures appear to foster beliefs and practices that can bring happiness in the midst of material poverty and its deprivations. Traditional wisdom and communal bonds and celebrations bring positive emotions and the sense of a meaningful life. Many who have engaged in lives of service among the poor have been surprised by the happiness to be found in unlikely places. The account of one writer's sojourn among the poorest of the poor in the slums of Calcutta was titled "Calcutta, the City of Joy." He received wisdom from those whose cultural resources were stronger than their misery. Working to survive the day made their lives worthwhile and meaningful. Living on the edge with beloved others dependent upon you activates interest and energetic effort. This was the lesson I learned in a small way while living with a large family below the poverty level. The fact that inner beliefs and practices can bring happiness gives more credence to claims that people can become happier. The pathways, attitudes, and practices that are found to be fruitful can be imitated. Resolve and commitment can be acknowledged as resources of the inner life and should never be underestimated.

In any discussion of the nature of happiness, it also should be noted how often religious faith and spirituality accompany the way to lasting happiness. It is a central challenge to believer and unbeliever alike. Does religious faith make you happy, and if so, how? More controversially, is it necessary to have a conscious, explicit faith in God and membership in a church to be happy? And is the happiness only for the next world? An examination of God and happiness uncovers and revives many more arguments to confront, which will be challenging and perhaps enjoyable.

Chapter 3

GOD AND HAPPINESS

Questions about God and happiness, so all-important for believers, include at least three. One, does God want human beings to be happy? Two, are humans able to become happy in this world? Three, is God in support of scientific and psychological programs for obtaining happiness? My affirmative answers to these questions—no surprise to anyone who has read this far—are the backbone or centerpiece or energizing fuel of this book on becoming happy. The previous introductory chapters on definitions and the following treatment of the science and application of happiness fly on the strength of my yes answers above. When resistance and hostility emerge to block the human pursuit of happiness, they are not sent by the Christian God.

My positive convictions about God's steadfast giving of happiness to humankind partly began during a memorable conversation I had thirty years ago with a colleague who became a Buddhist nun. My formerly Catholic friend was a medical doctor who had become a bioethical philosopher before going off to join a monastery. She told me that she had left the church to become a Buddhist because "it was the only religion that promised happiness in this life." "Oh!" I replied. "Really?" I was too flummoxed to muster an objection on the spot and only managed to say, "But wait a minute. Didn't St. Teresa say that all the way to heaven is heaven?"

This brief encounter along with many others during my resolutely secular training in a psychology PhD program started me down the road to books on joy, happiness, and suffering—or should I say up the path to positive psychology's optimistic claims that persons can become happy? In writing on the interaction of theology and psychological science I draw upon my academic education, my life experiences, and a half century's study and practice of Christianity. However, it is safe to say that many Christian believers, including many fellow Catholics, would not agree with my above affirmations. Nor do all psychologists approve of the science of happiness or positive psychology's proposed interventions promising a happier state. My approach to God and happiness may be judged as too broad and interdisciplinary in scope, and much too optimistic. Here, of course, I cannot hope to convince the opposition, but I can offer a brief for my affirmative stand.

In order to start on an irenic note, I think it is true that all within Christianity proclaim the gospel message as good news for humankind. Christianity teaches that God is love, and in the divine loving-kindness God in Christ saves the world. It can be agreed also that not all religious beliefs have been so sanguine. Many human beings have believed that the ultimate spiritual reality is a malevolent force. Shakespeare's despairing verses give voice to such a dark cry of despair: "We are to the gods as flies to wanton boys, they kill us for their sport."

The perceived hostility of all-powerful supernatural forces can produce crippling anxiety and a sense of helplessness. Such religious beliefs have led individuals and groups to sacrifice human victims in order to placate the gods. Human bodies have been tortured and killed in order to secure the safety and order of the tribe or kingdom. Compared to such horrific worldviews and practices—"The horror, the horror"—a divine indifference on the part of the gods can appear relatively benign. The Greek deities of Mount Olympus were, on the whole, neither consistently hostile nor invariably friendly. Human sacrifices might be required on special occasions, to procure a fair wind to sail to Troy, but the gods might also freely help individuals they favored. However, if humans got in the way of a divine agenda, the unfortunates could be destroyed or wantonly exploited. Individuals or groups were never freed from the fear that they might offend supernatural powers. Is this ever the case in the modern era?

Anxieties over placating demonic spirits may still waft around the edges of scientifically advanced societies. Semiserious, half-examined beliefs in occult forces can be found here and there. But such beliefs or worries hardly trouble the educated elites who have internalized dominant secular worldviews. No Western political leader would consider that his war plans were in peril from the ill will of supernatural forces, although many other kinds of anxieties over the unknown might exist. Often the lack of any morally committed faith provokes alarm over public morale and behavior. After all, nonreligious thinkers frequently voice a nihilism asserting the nonexistence of any ultimate meaning for human life. "We come from nothing, are going nowhere and have no ultimate purpose for our lives."

A default secular agnosticism asserts that all of human life is determined by probabilities, chance occurrences, and the impersonal laws of science. Humans who are happy are the chance products of their genes, blind fortune, and moral luck. In any event human happiness is fleeting and inexorably cut short by decline, degeneration, and death. Only the self-deceived and childish could claim that a God of love creates humans for endless happiness. Optimistic religious views are dismissed by "realists" (i.e., happiness pessimists) as delusional wish fulfillments. Yet Christians continue to believe and assert the good news.

God Wants Humans to Be Happy—Even If They Don't Believe or Offer Worship

Christians commit themselves to believing in one God who is the maker of heaven and earth and all things visible and invisible. In a continuous divine drama, God who is love creates, sustains, renews, and brings a good creation to a final fulfillment of eternal happiness. Humans are invited, but never coerced, to participate in God's life as members of God's family. The ultimate goal of life is to celebrate a communal feast of love and happiness with God's beloved community forever. Believers in the good news respond with continual thanks and praise. At each celebratory Eucharistic ritual meal the priest and people joyfully proclaim, "Happy are those who are called to your table." Hebrew psalms and Christian words of gladness ring out in the liturgical rites of the church. The good news "restores the joy of our youth," inspiring our spirits to "magnify the Lord" and to "rejoice always." Early church members were so filled with the spirit of joy that observers thought they were drunk on wine. And no wonder.

Jesus Christ is praised by his Christian disciples as the God-man who liberates and delivers the world through his saving life, his steadfast loving death, and his resurrection. He as the firstfruits of God's renewed creation and as fully God and fully human, empowers his brothers and sisters to become God's adopted family living in abundant joy. God's Holy Spirit is given through Christ and gives birth to humans who can live in loving communion and joy with God and man. This Christian vision of God giving happiness to humans produces a deepened and expanded foundation to the definition of happiness: true and lasting happiness is to live in, with, and through God's love and joy. The emotional, heart-lifting, transcendent peak experiences of happiness that humans have are recognized as God-given. Human hearts burn within when in the presence of God. Deep meaning occurs in human experiences of happiness since they reflect and share in God's own joy. With God as its divine source, happiness participates in the infinite. The communal relationships and active creative engagements that engender human happiness are not limited by space and time. Even fleeting joys participate in eternal reality and are not lost at death.

The gifts of creation's happiness incorporate and induce humans into God's divine liveliness. Persons are right to pursue happiness and welcome it enthusiastically. Happiness is not only a foretaste and pledge of a future fulfillment but a present participation in the energy of God's loving joy and divine yes. But a person who gratefully accepts this good news may still confront nagging questions: "How can this be, and why is it so? Why does God want humans to know and enjoy God forever? What is man that thou art mindful of him?" Humans can recognize that

God is an ineffable mystery transcending human understanding, but they still dare to inquire into divine purposes for humanity and the universe. Saint Augustine said that even to say that God is ineffable is already to say too much. True, to be silent in awe before the Mystery or *mysterium tremendum* is appropriate homage. But more can be inspired. Augustine himself wrote over a million words always trying to understand the ultimate truth of things, since he believed that a loving God also reveals Godself to humanity and seeks to be known intimately. Augustine says that God is closer to us than we are to ourselves.

Moreover, Christianity proclaims that humans made in the image of God have been given reason and intelligence in order to seek God as Truth. Faith seeks understanding confident of God's blessings on the quest. The innate human drive to know is God-given. God as love reveals Godself in God's self-bestowal of creation and communicates with persons. "I am who am," says Yahweh to Moses. Moses, it should be remembered, was amazed at the sight of the burning bush and so intensely curious that he willingly approached to look and stayed to listen.

As in the Hebrew story, God seeks to be known personally to individuals and groups of humans, but God also moves in the creation from the inside out. God is known as the ground of all being and source of all possibility. While God is recognized as the deepest energy of the world, God is also revealed as a benevolent God who is more passionately loving than mother, father, friend, lover, or spouse.

When these revealed Christian truths are affirmed it can be understood why God wants humans to be happy whether they explicitly offer worship or not. God is love and joy and truth, and divine love desires to share joyful truth with the beloved creation. God, being God, delights in giving, receiving, and relating with all who exist—not out of need but from exuberant, excessive, dynamic plenitude. If God possesses far more than any and all imagined perfections there can be no divine happiness deficits to be filled up. More specifically, the trinitarian God of Christianity exists in divinely three-persons unity in communion, eternally giving and receiving love and joy. The energy of mutual loving and relating generates creativity and overflows into creation. God is a never-ending fountain of creativity, a wellspring of novelty and surprise.

Most wonderfully, human beings are created in God's image and incorporated into the divine fullness of life through responses of loving communion. As the ancient theological maxim expresses it, God becomes man so that man can become God. Other names for becoming Godlike are being "adopted" into God's family, "divinization," "theosis," and best of all, the old English word "engodded." Humans are drawn into the life of the Trinity, and become eternally happy in the infinite loving communion. These high and mighty theological reflections on divinization express the essence of the good news in ways that may seem abstract. The faithful can, however, dimly intuit their deep truths by thinking of how much they love their own children, and how passionately they desire for them to grow up and be happy adult members of the family.

Clearly, too, with the astounding ineffable wonder of God's loving generosity, there can be no question of earning or deserving such love and joyfulness. God's giving of Godself goes far beyond all reason or merit. No one is refused the living water who comes to the well. How then should humans respond? How can they respond here and now?

Humans Can Become Happy in This World

When we move from asking "Why?" to the question of "How does becoming or transformation work?" more differences of opinion and complexities emerge among Christians. While all the faithful may agree that, yes, God wants humans to be happy and enjoy God's love and happiness forever, the faithful can differ on the prerequisites and timing of events. Those holding to the most strict and pessimistic views would deny that humans can be happy in this world and maintain that God's joy can only be experienced in the next life. All of the generously given sources of happiness existing in the creation and innately evolved human nature are ignored, discounted, or despised as dangerous. This fallen earthly life among corrupted sinners is a sinkhole of evil and may at best be endured. Such dark visions of the human condition are often matched by strict and severe theological strictures regarding the requirements for receiving the gifts of salvation.

Heaven and its happiness are limited to those select few who explicitly confess Jesus Christ as their Lord and Savior and are baptized into his body, the church. To successfully attain heaven, baptized church members must fulfill the commandments, repent and confess all sins committed, and do appropriate penance. Perseverance until death is required, and last rites must be duly received. After dying, judgment, and purgatorial purification, the faithful can finally enter into God's fullness of joy.

Not surprisingly, those holding strict and pessimistic versions of the corruption of human and earthly life claim that few are saved. The majority of sinful humans reject and disobey God's commands, and thus justly deserve to be damned for their sins. A denial of God in this life is judged to be damnable and irrevocable, with no second chances possible.

Optimistic Christian thinkers, by contrast, are hopeful and confident that all will be saved, even if after much turmoil and travail. I, for one, can envision an expanded purgatorial learning process beginning at death and ending in eventual salvation. Why should God's loving powers of persuasion and divine pedagogy be underestimated, especially when God has all the time in the world and can call upon the saints and friends of God as eager helpers? As the old song goes, "Love will find a way." To which pessimists respond, "Too late," and "Nevermore."

While strict versions of the Christian story agree that refusals of God in this life are irrevocable, they can differ over the severity of the consequences. Is it eternal damnation in agonies of extreme suffering or a withering away into nothingness? Orthodox Christians once endorsed a Jonathan Edwards scenario of heaven in which the shrieking of the damned in the tormenting fires of hell gave joyful satisfaction to the saints rejoicing in God's justice. Then there were other Dante-inspired visions of exquisitely calibrated punishments for different kinds and degrees of wickedness. Today in modern Catholic theological thought, the faithful are instructed that hell should not be thought of as a place, but as a condition in which God is absent. Graphic depictions of hellfires and torture can now be seen as making concrete the symbolic imagery used in scripture's apocalyptical literary passages. Gospel references in parables to hell's torments of thirst amid flames and anguished "wailing and gnashing of teeth" contributed to concrete conceptualization of hell's unhappiness.

Damnation in hell, however literal, concrete, or painfully envisioned, is not accidental or arbitrary in mainstream Christianity but the just consequence of an individual's free rejection of the love of God and love of neighbor. "Non serviam" (I will not serve), asserts proud Lucifer in Milton's *Paradise Lost*. These words of defiance are repeated by Stephen Dedalus in James Joyce's *Ulysses*, who joins a long line of fictional protagonists rejecting and rebelling against God. And since art imitates life, many rejections and denunciations of God have been proclaimed in the past and present. Currently, a new crop of crusading atheists are stating that God is not great, or indeed, God is not. They contend that human reason and dignity necessitate the rejection of false and toxic religious beliefs. Their books, lectures, and demonstrations are popular and profitable, offering their own versions of human happiness.

On the other hand, equally bestselling literary and media descriptions of heaven and happiness flood the cultural scene. Traditional depictions of heaven employ biblical images and symbols; heaven is described as a shining celestial city, a king's marriage feast, or the holy mountain sheltering the peaceable kingdom. More modern images of heavenly happiness may employ technological flourishes. Curiously, many current depictions of the heavenly afterlife are amorphously vague, with few clues as to where or whether God exists. Much of the popular near-death literature is filled with roseate floating auras of joy and shining lights at the end of the tunnel. Of course, these are *near*-death experiences, and the person has to turn back to earth at the last minute.

In contrast, no one could think medieval depictions of the Last Judgment to be lacking detailed and specific doctrinal content about God's whereabouts. The blissful souls of the saved ascend toward God, depicted as two men and a bird, and the miserable damned descend into hell's demonic torture chambers presided over by Satan. The only existing ambiguities in earlier visions of the afterlife involved the in-between state of souls in limbo. Limbo existed as a pleasant, restful place where good pagans, like Virgil, and unbaptized babies could abide. Residents of limbo were thought to be deprived of the fullest measure of Christian happiness through no fault of their own for being outside the church. In the last decade, limbo for unbaptized babies has been doctrinally disappeared (or reinterpreted) and replaced by a general reliance on God's mercy. These changes follow a general retreat of religion from concrete, narrow, and punitive pictures of the afterlife. Yet not every religious believer has moved in this direction. Fundamentalists of all persuasions still defend literal and exclusive versions of heavenly happiness and hell. Christian fundamentalists preach against liberal thinkers whom they see as betraying God's truth in their lax offers of cheap grace.

In rebuttal, optimistic Christian thinkers steadfastly insist on the infinitely merciful and inclusive love of God who desires human happiness on earth and in heaven. They point to the fact that Christian doctrines and symbols inevitably evolve and develop over the generations. Development of Christian doctrine is affirmed as the work of the Holy Spirit who leads the pilgrim church on its way to God. The church has to be a learning church, moving toward deeper and more comprehensive understandings of God's word. As historians and theologians analyze the long centuries of Christian church teachings and tradition, it becomes clear that the church can preserve the core gospel message and simultaneously evolve interpretations of what is essential and what is transitory and culture bound. The understanding of God's love and mercy is steadily becoming more central, more universally pervasive, and more readily identified with God's gifts of earthly happiness. It can always be affirmed that the *fullest* human bliss will be a complete union with God beyond death and sin, but this "more beyond, and not yet" need not diminish the happiness of the "here and now, already."

Theological reinterpretations have emerged to explain how universal saving grace operates for those outside the institutional church.

"Baptism by desire," for instance, is accepted as a path to heavenly joy and salvation. Or an individual's fundamental option toward the good can be effective for salvation. Indeed, God's saving joy can be given to good persons who may never have heard of Christ. Humans of every age and place can receive God's happiness if they abide by the innate and fundamental laws of goodness written on the human heart. More important, perhaps, is the mitigating idea that those who appear to have heard and rejected God's call may be influenced by circumstances that make it impossible for them to actually hear or accept the word. In the past these individuals were quaintly described as being "invincibly ignorant," and thus not fully responsible for their refusals. An optimist can take this thought further and envision unbelieving societies with so much interference and noise that only at the moment of death can each person encounter Christ as he is, speaking words that can be heard. The beginning of God's next-life remedial efforts perhaps? Still greater optimists might identify a way to God through disbelief.

Other understandings of God's universal inclusive mercy appear in the church's growing appreciation of other religions as valid responses to God's spirit. Growing knowledge of other faiths has encouraged the growth of ecumenical movements. These Christian overtures spring from a surging confidence in the work of the Holy Spirit who is always and everywhere drawing humankind into God's love and truth. The growth of worldwide expressions of spirituality is generated by the life-giving Holy Spirit. Christians proclaiming the unfailing loving-kindness of God's merciful inclusiveness also point to the Gospel accounts of Christ's life and work.

Jesus Christ embodies the truth that God's loving forgiveness and healing are offered to all: the foreigner, the tax gatherer, the leper and lunatic, outcast women, mothers and children, and the exploited poor. "A bruised reed I will not break or a flickering wick extinguish," reads a prophetic verse applied to Christ's ministry. Christ's disciples are told to extend God's love and mercy to everyone, with no exceptions, even offering forgiveness and love to enemies. Justice must reign, but God's love and forgiveness are always present; justice and mercy will kiss. The

Gospel proclaims that Christ has opened a door for humankind that no one can close.

In the same way that God pours forth gifts on all, the believing and the unbelieving, God calls all humankind to goodness and good work. Unbelievers and the nonreligious possess the universal God-given Spirit and are drawn to God as Truth. The moral capacity of conscience is a universal gift. Unbelievers can listen to the innate moral dictates written on their hearts and in their minds and follow their consciences' ethical pull toward truth and morality. In our secular age, with the spread of unbelief, individuals can live good moral lives without explicit religious allegiance. When unbelievers live upright lives according to their conscience they can become happy and sustain happiness.

God's Spirit of truth and love permeate the creation from within and generate virtue and happiness. One apt scriptural symbol of God's influence is that of yeast, which enables the bread to rise. Other modern symbols of the pervasive influence of God's grace are the power of magnetic attraction, or more cosmically, astronomy's mysterious great attractor, drawing galaxies toward it across the universe. Teilhard de Chardin saw all of the evolutionary processes of the universe as ascending to an omega point, or final unifying fulfillment, in Christ. The light of the world attracts, illuminates, enkindles, warms, and delights human beings in truth and love. Heart speaks to heart and engenders joy.

Work, too, as already noted here, is an innate and universal source of human happiness. Always and everywhere effective work brings its intrinsic rewards and satisfactions. Humans made in the image of God experience joy in creating and working to make things happen. There is a joy in accomplishing goals, or in having the Godlike dignity of being a cause. Psychologists now identify and study absorbing states of goal-oriented activity called flow and speak of the rewards arising from self-efficacy. Theologians express and explain this truth by claiming that God gives humans the privilege of acting as "created cocreators." The call to stewardship given in the garden of Eden consists of far more than the dressing of the garden and naming of the animals.

The first disciples heard Christ tell them that he works, that God his Father works, and that they will do greater works than he. Jesus, in doing God's work, receives an intense happiness that he describes as his meat and drink, and bringing God's fire to ignite the world. Jesus works eagerly because he knows that for this he was born. Pursuing a unique calling brings joy, but even carrying out more ordinary and common tasks with care produces satisfactions and happiness. Work has innate rewards but possesses deep and positive meanings for Christians who believe that their activities as created cocreators are participating in God's work of renewing the world. "Whatever you do whether in word or work, do for the glory of God," says Saint Paul. Everything, whether large or small, done in love, counts in bringing the creation to fulfillment. When joined with Christ's ongoing work, all efforts and offerings contribute to the transforming process. Even failures and sufferings are effectively incorporated into Christ's saving work, which encompassed an obedience described as "ready for anything." Christ's whole life—joys and triumphs of love along with sufferings, betrayal, torture, and failures—gave birth to a new resurrected humankind. Such Christian beliefs about the useful offering of each human life, no matter what amount of joy or sorrow it contains, has brought a sense of purpose and great happiness to Christian believers.

Pursuing and completing purposive goals makes all individuals happy. Babies and children reveal this innate and intrinsic delight in the activity of absorbing play. The child's enjoyment of playing or their love affair with the world grows into the adult's love of accomplishment and competence. Admittedly, experiences of alienated enslaved labor can be a curse as they inflict great suffering on individuals. Oppressed workers have been literally worked to death in misery. The gulag's freezing labor camps come to mind, or the harrowing mistreatment of the poor in factories or mines. Yet the distortions of slavery and wage slavery do not disprove the reality that individuals and groups find happiness in doing, making, and accomplishing goals. Even in the gulag, rare spirits found experiences of happiness. Humans have evolved the innate positive emotion of interest and curiosity; they always and everywhere become happy in discovering, problem solving, inventing, and making things happen alone and with others. Novelty attracts and compels interest just as familiarity produces contentment. Engaging in effective activity generates happiness, and so does pleasurable and joyful rest and contentment.

God gives human beings freedom and power to work and act on their own initiative. The giving and nurturing activity that empowers others is called "enabling power" since it inspires others to act and effectively develop their own capacities. It is different from the kind of coercive power that dominates and controls through external force and fear of punishment. The logic of domination aims to subjugate others by force and compel conformity to the powerful agent's will. Enabling or nurturing power is more enduring since it works through free internalization and cooperation that does not require coercive surveillance.

Enabling power creates growth in others as well as engendering the bonds that maintain families or groups. God the loving Creator is eternally nurturing and calling humans to become co-heirs and adopted children by growing up into Christ their head. This growing up into adulthood in freedom, as every parent can attest, can be uneven, intermittently regressive, and far from tranquil. To give others freedom to fulfill their own potential means accepting the risks of moral failures, missteps, sufferings, and sin. The different capacities that evolved in human beings can war against each other instead of working together.

Yet in freely exercising agency, humans can become mature, integrated sons and daughters of God, not conforming slaves or puppets. The familiar story of Pinocchio's adventures and misadventures in becoming a real-live boy is an instructive fable. The freedom that is necessary for growing also opens possibilities for setbacks. Freely rejecting the moral pull of conscience produces increasing deformation (of more than the length of your nose) as well as misery for self and others—in both the short and long run. Proud assertions of self-will that reject God and the good produce hardness of heart and isolation. As one looks at the list of the seven deadly sins, they each reject a good virtue that leads to integrated happiness, and each produces a special form of misery and disintegration.

The gospel and innate moral goodness call humans to happiness and joy. By freely imitating Christ's nonviolent nurturing power of love and truth, humans become happy. Christ says of himself that he is humble and meek of heart and that the meek will be deeply happy and blessed. They also inherit the earth. At the same time Christ claims authority to proclaim God's truth in his teaching, his healing, and his merciful forgiving of sins. Do God's truth and perfection include a divine humility?

The provocative idea of the humility of God is now explored in evolutionary theology. God's humility can be discerned in the way God becomes human and gives freedom and power to humans to become cocreators of life in the creation. Have we misinterpreted the meaning of omnipotence as a divine perfection? Renouncing coercive power and giving freedom to others to create themselves is an ultimate act of love and humility. Certainly, in Christ's living, loving, suffering, and dying, the saving action is not modeled on that of a conquering Roman emperor declared divine, but on that of a mother, father, brother, sister, and friend. The relationship and exercise of Christ's power are those of the inspiration, attraction, and love that binds together friends. "I have called you friends," says Christ.

The near-unbelievable news of Christianity is that a nurturing God plays a win-win game. In the creation, giving and loving are also receiving—and this mutuality and union bring happiness. As in the description of the love generated in the Trinity, giving, loving, and receiving produce joy. This ultimate template for all reality is reproduced and instanced in the way human happiness is engendered by giving in friendship, sexual love, family nurturing, and creative engaged work. In losing self for love you find yourself, and in giving you receive—frequently receiving back tenfold of the gift. When giving and loving are the source of happiness, then Christ's words to his disciples are confirmed: "My joy I give you, which no one can take from you."

Christ describes the deeply happy life he lives and offers in the address and teachings of the Beatitudes. The famous words tell his disciples that those who accept his truth will be blessed or deeply happy when they live a life of loving and giving. Whatever the circumstances, whether favorable, unfavorable, or dire, Christians can find happiness in the meaning and effectiveness of steadfast loving, empathetic mourning, merciful humility, continual truth seeking, effortful peacemaking, and participation in Christ's friendship during persecution for the truth. Again the most remarkable character of the promises is that even suffering can produce deep happiness when offered in union with Christ's saving love and work. Losing one's life or taking up one's cross in loving service can lead to joy.

Who or what external circumstance could take away a joy produced by loving, giving, and working? This is why Christ assures his followers that his yoke is light and that he gives rest to the weary and living water to the thirsty. Christ is recognized as the rock following the people, who bestows a wellspring of living water flowing from the heart. And what is more fully joy-producing than living water that quenches thirst and brings life to the desert?

Christ's words, like his life, contradict the world's usual assumptions about happiness. A fearful, anxious people threatened by death and loss can believe that they must fight to grasp happiness by selfish, assertive, competitive, and self-protective aggression. Many will seek happiness in riches, in dominating power, and in high status for self and kin. Yet Christ teaches that blessedness comes from self-giving love, altruistic action, and humble, creative friendship and engaged cooperation. Christ's words are proclaimed authoritatively as the real governing truths of God's creation; they will not pass away. When humans accept and live in this truth they become happy. God's goodness is freely given to all. Christ's words are guiding truths that lead to the narrow, but brightly illuminated, gate of life and joy. The path is God-given and revealed in faith, but all those who find happiness travel the familiar road. Those who reject these truths inflict familiar sufferings upon themselves. These natural laws of human psychological life do mean that a moral refraining from harm-doing is a requirement for happiness. A certain level of morality in an attentive effort to stay on the path leads to lasting happiness. This adherence to nonviolence and loving-kindness is universal and provides the root explanation of the convergence of different religions and wisdom traditions. And is not the convergence also evident in the psychological science of happiness as well? I think so.

Today's Christians can be gratified, if not surprised, to find that many revealed spiritual truths of the faith are being supported by new scientific researches on happiness and human nature. While the next chapter on the science of happiness discusses these developments more fully, a few points can be previewed here as theologically relevant. Neuroscientists, for instance, studying the complexities of the evolved human brain find that acts of altruism generate emotionally positive feelings that correlate with activated reward signals in the brain. This finding is named the helper principle and helps confirm that human altruism exists. Similar research into forgiveness shows by various reliable measures that actively forgiving enemies and past injuries produces feelings of happiness, as well as improving different measures of physical health. As we shall see, large-scale survey studies repeatedly show that loving families, circles of friends, religious worship, and altruistic work correlate with reports of happiness, along with higher measures of health and longevity.

Humans also appear to have evolved with innate moral capacities and possess brains that produce consciousness and flexible, self-aware self-control of attention and behavior. Thinking, feeling, and behaving can be directed by unimpaired mature human beings. This consciousness and agency provide resources for becoming happy. Individuals can choose and make efforts to be good, to love others, and to give themselves to altruistic and creative activities. Intelligent self-awareness can avoid and solve many problems, beginning with one's own behavior. Self-regulation of emotion is also possible in an incredibly complex brain organized in multisystemic ways.

No one yet understands the brain and consciousness, but it does appear that the positive and negative emotional systems are separate and can be activated separately and together. Joy and sorrow, or happiness and mourning, can coexist, as the Beatitudes and Gospel truths proclaim. This human capacity for simultaneously or quickly succeeding positive and negative emotional responses can explain how martyrs could go singing to their deaths full of joy in their union with Christ, while undergoing agonizing tortures. The complicated, evolved subsystems and levels of quicksilver streams of consciousness and emotion can also help explain how a person could experience deeper or more lasting emotions of happiness while superficially experiencing transitory feelings of negative emotions. Can there be a happily married person who has not experienced moments of irritation and anger?

But again there may be certain limits in the rough natural laws of human emotions. It appears that while joy and certain kinds of suffering can coexist, joy may not be able to coexist with highly aroused negative emotions of hate, envy, disgust, contempt, guilt, and shame. Certain emotional torments of raging envy, lust, greed, or proud contempt that dominate consciousness can isolate selves from the sources of happiness. Emotional flooding or emotional wildfires of negative emotions can leave no room for joy. Empathetic suffering, in contrast, is compatible with joy because it unites with the other in benevolence; it enhances the self's altruistic relationship to the other and receives the fruit of loving. Those who mourn with others will be comforted in the same way.

Another theologically relevant direction of recent research is the focus on the power of positive emotions for healing, undoing, or overcoming destructive and traumatic experiences (more on this in later chapters). Just as present forgiveness of past injuries can be important in emotional healing, present happiness can also undo trauma. New relationships, forgiveness, and love can overcome the agonies and anxieties of being a victim and erase raging desires for revenge. Love casts out fear. The memory of past sufferings can be emotionally defused; the sting is removed. Those who are fulfilled and rejoice in the present can deactivate and reshape the patterns and configurations of the past.

Such an understanding of the healing powers of positive emotions for memories has theological relevance for Christian hope. That such healings and change are possible even in this life gives a model for transformation in the life to come. It is instructive to see humans finding happiness and healing their past through finding a deeper, broader, more intensely positive outlook in a joyful present. In an ongoing story, the past and old wounds can be healed as present positive emotions reshape the pattern and force of memories. How much more it will be likely that God and the beloved community's joy in the life to come can heal innocent sufferings and frustrated lives on earth. And cannot the wounds and deformations springing from sin also be healed by transformations? Is this what is meant by the comforting words, "Your sins, although scarlet, will be washed white as snow"?

The glorious promise is given that nothing is wasted, no victim un-justified and transformed, all the unfulfilled lives can be lived when death and time are no longer limitations. New evolutionary theologians also widen their concerns beyond the human future. They assert that all the pain and suffering of sentient animals throughout evolution's competitive and selective processes will be healed in the final fulfillment. The Christian message of salvation can be expanded to affirmations that God loves each creature; no sparrow falls without God's concern. Divine empathy and suffering with all the pain of God's creatures are affirmed. But to see God only as a fellow sufferer does not heal wounds or bring curtailed and painful lives to fruition. The preyed-upon sentient animal would need more in order to take part in God's final fulfillment of the creation as very good. Sentient beings will also participate in the new resurrected life in their creaturely way. Cooperation, harmony, and integration of all life in the cosmic Christ who holds all things together can be seen as the greatest birthing of happiness.

Evolutionary consciousness can be seen as a gift from science for many reasons, but most innovatively it encourages an appreciation of all God's creatures. The goodness and value of prerational or irrational human lives cut short or deformed by impairments can be celebrated. Fetal lives lost, infants who die, the profoundly retarded, and the mentally impaired are included in a saving fulfillment in which all creaturely life is brought to fruition. The conflicting drives of all living and natural systems to survive and persist will be brought into harmony. The lion will lie down with the lamb, and a child will play with the asp. Only with such integration, restoration, and harmony of all life could self-conscious animals like ourselves be wholly fulfilled. Christian imagina-tions in the past could see paradise regained by Christ but had less to say about animal fulfillment in the last day. (Angels yes, chimpanzees no?) Perhaps Saint Francis when he preached to the birds and the wolves was a prophetic figure in the growth of Christian ecological and evolutionary consciousness.

While humans have the potent and wonderful gift of imagining and thinking about what is not present, it can still be a challenge to imagine a fulfilled happiness with God and the beloved community that is not visible. It is reassuring that Saint Paul says that no eye has seen nor ear heard nor mind imagined what a loving God has prepared for the future. Intelligent humans through much negative and positive experience have figured out that just because we are too limited to imagine something new and invisible—as, for instance, in science—it can still be true. God is known as a God of surprises. No one of my generation could have imagined the new scientific discoveries that have taken place and changed our world. Seeing is not necessary for believing in the unseen, or a yet undiscovered future. Could a dinosaur imagine a lion or a fetus imagine life after birth?

From the moment of birth, however, an infant participates in the reality that human emotions are contagious. Positive and negative emotions are both intuitively and automatically transmitted in an empathetic flash. In a group, fear and anger are communicated instantly. But positive emotions as with laughter are also contagious; a baby's laughter, for instance, lifts the heart of all in earshot. Happiness is as fully contagious as anger and fear. Those who can abide in God's joyful presence can be happy or, to coin a phrase, felicitously infectious. Delight begets delight. Gratitude for present and past joys produces more happiness. Calling to mind all the past and present God-given goods of a life can engender and escalate into what some have called a positive high of gratitude. In sum, happiness can be engendered and magnified by repetition. A plethora of human experiences produces and begets more human happiness: physical pleasures, aesthetic delights, intellectual discoveries, as well as working and problem solving. Joy abounds in worship, love, friendship, and playful humor, and is perennially produced by poetry, art, music, dance, nature, altruism, and combinations of all of the above. The plenitude of pleasure and happiness exists in the creation and participates in God's own joy.

The promise is that at the end-time, symbolically depicted as the new Jerusalem or the coming kingdom, the beloved community of God's creation will rejoice in gladness forever. Every tear will be wiped away, and there will be no more mourning, pain, or death. When a God of love is all in all, there will be no more waste or stunted, frustrated, un-fulfilled, and miserable lives. Sorrow will be no more.

In the creation's ongoing journey to the end-time, or the new heaven and new earth, God can be trusted to be sustaining, continually creat-ing, and interpenetrating all of reality while generously empowering and cooperating with free, created cocreators. While the ultimate victory is already won through Christ's resurrection, humans live in the not-yet time of the great birthing process. Scripture speaks of our good creation as still undergoing its final birthing process, groaning in travail, awaiting its final deliverance with humanity. Humanity is given an important role in bringing God's new life into completion, and in the process it can participate in the joy of the present and future victory. Indeed Christians are called to increase joy and happiness in the creation as they love, serve, liberate, and relieve suffering. Seeking to love God with all their hearts and minds, and their neighbors as themselves, persons receive God's joy. In the midst of God's great birthing event, and in their own growing up, humans trust in the future outcome and celebrate in joy. Present joys and gladness in ecstasy or contentment witness to the great yes.

Chapter 4

A SCIENCE OF HAPPINESS?

A new science of happiness has arrived. Unlikely as it may sound, scientists, mainly of a social psychological persuasion, aim to add scientific know-how to the pursuit of happiness. This is not too surprising since modern science possesses immense authority and keeps expanding its reach. As two of the most prominent happiness researchers put it, science "is now expanding our understanding and control of the subjective world." Can it be true? If this move succeeds, a new frontier will be opened in the pursuit of happiness.

Already science has grown into a huge, multileveled, broad-branched empire; it covers vast territories employing different theories, methods, and tools to take on the universe in a fair, even thrilling fight. Its aura of authority is built upon its amazing successes in producing reliable and valid knowledge that transforms our lives. The essence of science was succinctly stated by Nobel physicist Richard Feynman: "Science is not fooling yourself." To this end scientists use rigorous methods to obtain the best information that is available. Precise empirical observations and quantifiable measurement are the key weapons in the struggle not to fool oneself, and control groups and statistics are added to the arsenal. A range of methods and statistical analyses help produce reliable results that other investigators can replicate. One of the great virtues and advantages of science and the scientific method is its built-in skepticism and use of doubt for self-correction. Science and Christianity both are in quest of Truth, with a capital T, which can be a hidden reality. They also share a healthy suspicion of the ways fallible humans find what they want to find. Scientists, like everyone else on earth, can make innocent errors and, worse still, sometimes give in to the temptation to cheat before being found out and excommunicated.

In today's science of happiness, several related agendas are in play. I am most interested in studies of individual happiness and finding out whether and how persons can intentionally become happy. These efforts include constructing therapeutic interventions and self-help guidance, and are closely related to the practice of psychotherapy. Other large-scale group investigations are equally central to the emerging science of happiness. Sociologically oriented research projects investigate the happiness of targeted populations by collecting data on their happiness, identified at times as "subjective well-being," "life satisfaction," "human flourishing," or general well-being. These different shadings of meaning tend to overlap.

Large-scale projects produce large amounts of information that can serve as a background for learning about individuals, but are particularly important for policy makers concerned with establishing institutional arrangements for different populations. Empirical group data on who is happy, and where, and under what kinds of social, political, economic, and cultural conditions can be helpful in setting goals for governmental decision making. Businesses and other institutions can also benefit from such general knowledge. Socially and politically oriented scientific research on happiness uses standard social scientific methods and highly technical statistical analyses. These studies are only considered innovative because they are aimed at happiness as a facet of the subjective world.

Social scientific research on a population's happiness or subjective well-being selects a large sample of subjects and seeks to find reliable and valid information on existing correlates. When economists join the team, they tend to bring along their term "utility" as an economics-speak description of happiness. Not surprisingly, economists want to include inquiries on productivity and income, along with the ways their distribution correlates with other measures of life satisfaction. The more variables that are measured, the more comprehensive the study—and the more expensive. The pertinent question is always, "How does this selected range of individual, social, and environmental variables correlate with measures of happiness?" Information in one recent, widely publicized study of the fifty states in the United States, appearing in the highly regarded journal *Science*, correlated measures of climate, air pollution, crime rates, taxes, traffic congestion, schools, and real estate prices with reported life satisfaction. In a comparison of the results on relative standings, Louisiana placed first among the states, and New York was last.

Since New York City is home to crowds of highly competitive, critical commentators on everything that matters, the bottom ranking of New York state rankled and was vigorously challenged. The results could only be seen as misleading to those who are certain of the compelling importance and magnetism of Manhattan and the Empire State. Quickly, skeptical questions appeared in the press criticizing the problematic methods and biases of social scientific research. Critics wanted to know which variables were selected and how were they weighted, along with the way the questions in polls and interviews were phrased. Objectors could also question the statistics used and complain about the practices of aggregating group data. The Big Apple's residents could not think that the response of residents in the far-off (and dull) reaches of upstate New York should be lumped in with them, or more technically have their responses equally weighted. Besides, goes another familiar refrain, there's the perennial difficulty of defining happiness satisfactorily. Perhaps New Yorkers are simply giving deeper, more realistic, and more honest responses to the complex realities of life satisfaction—just because they live in such a stimulating environment. After all, people flock to New York City from all over America and the world. Who immigrates to Louisiana, except "to see my Susyanna sing Polly wolly doodle all the day"?

Critiques and skeptical reservations about social science research are very familiar. Critics often have a valid point, for biased and erroneous assumptions can creep into a study's design. Increasingly, too, scientific controversies are appearing over the appropriate statistical methods that should be used. Is a statistically significant finding really significant, as in meaningful? Should any present finding be taken as definitive or only temporary? Scientists are committed to openness and doubt; this means constant correction, revision, and rapid dating of studies. However, in my estimation these problems can be discounted; well-done and careful studies are being designed and admirably carried out. They produce accurate and useful results; factual information serves to correct bias, personal impressions, and anecdotal evidence. "Data" is not the plural of "anecdote." Skilled social scientists work long and hard to devise reliable methods and analyses that avoid confounding errors. They use controlled cross-modal checking and replication, and hold to the highest standards of experimental research to obtain reliable and valid results. Only occasionally is it garbage in, garbage out.

Happiness research studies are no different from other inquiries; they are as valuable as the theory, designs, methods, and analytic statistical tools employed. Group data on subjective well-being can be collected by multimethod measures, polls, surveys, interviews, questionnaires, rating scales, peer interviews, longitudinal studies, content analysis, unobtrusive objective measures, and combinations of all of the above and more. Sherlock Holmes is the model; he was able to attend to everything that was on the scene, as well as what wasn't, like the dog that doesn't bark in the night. It takes skill and ingenuity to accurately outwit fallible human beings responding in self-reports on their subjective states. People can misunderstand the questions; always respond with the highest, lowest, or middle score; or be influenced by the demand characteristics of the setting or a reaction to a specific researcher. Individuals can also forget, misremember, exaggerate, intentionally lie, or be genuinely self-deceived. And the basic operating assumption in happiness studies, which is often criticized, is that people are able to give reliable scores and know how happy they are overall. The scientific gold standard also demands that corroborating information be gathered from different sources in order to triangulate, cross-check, and verify findings. Fortunately, in the academic, peer-reviewed, scientific happiness research that is published, seasoned researchers using reliable measures and methods—along with sophisticated computer programs—can produce robust and credible results.

Peer-reviewed results of happiness studies are published not only in older premier academic journals like *Science*, but in newly established publications such as the *Journal of Happiness Studies*. New disciplines and interdisciplinary programs appear in elite colleges with academic happiness specialists. Moreover, at least one international center for happiness studies has been founded in Holland that provides access to huge collections of research data. There, one can find indexes, databases, journal articles, bibliographies, and other relevant social science collections. When so many research studies are available, they can be collated, organized, and analyzed to produce rankings in happiness scores—for countries, regions, states, selected populations, and other groups. While it is intellectually risky to quantify, aggregate, and compare different sets of methodologically disparate studies, researchers do it anyway. National rankings naturally draw media attention. Who isn't curious about where their own state, nation, or regional group places in the happiness sweepstakes? Humans are a hypersocial and competitive species; they are always sensitive to hierarchies and relative status, and they consume lists of the ten best and ten worst of everything. Every fifth-grade girl can report on which clique ranks where in the middle-school social circles. I was talking to my granddaughter about the high school social scene and, following up on her description of the boy gangs, asked her who the mean girls were. "We're all mean girls," she replied with a straight face, putting an end to the investigation. But I had already gotten an inside picture of the local ranking system this year.

Unfortunately, year after year America ranks below other developed Western countries in happiness scores. Just as regularly the top places go to Scandinavian countries and Switzerland. A *New Yorker* ad announced in eye-catching large print, "Discover Denmark, the World's Happiest Nation." In tiny print at the bottom, the ad says, "Come see for yourself why Danes are routinely polled as the happiest people on earth." Other polling routinely finds that the bottom ranks are filled by poverty-stricken, strife-torn failed states, whose populations suffer from hunger, disease, crime, civil war, totalitarian dictatorships, corruption, and natural disasters. Yet poverty isn't the only factor at work. The correlation of monetary wealth with "psychological wealth" or the "ultimate currency" of happiness is not a simple linear relationship. Once above the poverty, destitution, and disaster levels, higher incomes don't automatically guarantee higher happiness scores. Certain oil-rich states, for instance, that lack democratic governments do not rank high on subjective well-being scores, despite luxurious lifestyles and high welfare provisions. Unhappiness, dissatisfaction, apathy, and cynicism are spawned by widespread corruption and an authoritarian disregard of equal human rights. Wealth does not make up for a population's lack of access to democratic governance.

In contrast, an open, just society with basic rights and guaranteed welfare provisions produces higher happiness scores. When you can trust the system, it is easier to trust the others who also have a stake in things; trust is key in preventing the corroding suspicion, envy, and cynicism that make a population miserable—however affluent. Morally it is encouraging news that objective, empirical studies show correlations between a society's practices of justice and equality and its levels of subjective happiness. Here the new science of happiness gives support to old philosophical and religious arguments that a commitment to the common good produces human flourishing. Happy societies, like Denmark, are built on established legal respect for the rights, dignity, and economic welfare of all its individual members. A test from a natural disaster, flood, or earthquake can also show democracies to be resilient. And what about social disasters? Some recent research on the U.S. population reveals that not having work, or widespread unemployment, decisively lowers collective happiness. Surely, this empirical finding has practical and policy implications for a democratic government.

Another intriguing result of happiness rankings shows that high levels of faith and explicit religious affiliations are not correlated with a society's level of happiness. The highly secularized countries in Scandinavia, along with Switzerland, continually have the highest scores for happiness but the lowest scores for religious belief and church affiliation. This outcome causes some puzzlement since in all other cross-cultural research on individuals, religious persons show the most happiness (as well as the highest rates of good health, marital and economic stability, altruism, and lowered anxiety). These paradoxical findings, it seems to me, could be resolved. If, for instance, the term "spiritual" is used as a personal descriptive category rather than the term "religious," which implies being a member of a religious institution, then the secularity of a society may be less clear-cut. As we can all attest, many people in modern societies say, "I am a spiritual person, but I'm not religious." Another thought that makes some sense is that the secularized Western democracies' just institutions and welfare benefits were built upon inherited legacies of Christian ideals that have been transformed into humanitarian values. In this view, secular humanism is living off the value fat remaining from past religious beliefs. Whether this analysis is true, there is little doubt that the scientific happiness research gives evidence that without humanistic moral values of justice and democracy, affluence alone can hardly ensure happiness and human flourishing.

In fact, affluence may even threaten the subjective well-being of developed societies, despite their democratic governments. Some researchers have found that the fast-paced way of life of economically productive populations can diminish happiness. The increasing number of consumer choices and active options of affluence can produce subjective tensions and stress. Choices and opportunities multiply, but the hours in each day remain the same. Did I, for instance, last week have to troll through a thousand lamps for sale on the Internet in order to purchase one? The constant time crunch of every day erodes the time spent on family life, friendship, leisure, and participation in community political and religious activities. The constant speeding up and future-oriented striving for higher and higher achievement impoverishes the quality of the present. Such pressures bring stress that accompany air pollution, excessive traffic, lengthy commuting times, higher mortgages, and more consumer debt. Does this highway lead back to Louisiana, where the culture lets the good times roll, and where slow cooking and living can still be found?

Health researchers worried about the side effects of the spread of Western lifestyles have noted other threats to global happiness from rising affluence. Stress from the developed world's competitive push bringing economic productivity can also bring Western diseases. Unhealthy diets of newly available fast foods encourage obesity and diseases such as heart ailments. Moreover, increasing global rates of depression and suicide do not spare affluent populations. The domain of public health is definitely another arena where the social science research on human flourishing and happiness can help countries to improve national policies. Governments can try to provide proactive policies and interventions that foster community and family support structures to actively increase happiness. A positive approach to activating human strengths and values can work proactively for mental health and flourishing, rather than reactive approaches focused upon treating mental illness after it has occurred. Social alienation and various forms of underactive languishing make individuals vulnerable to illness. As the saying goes, happiness and joy are the greatest antidotes for depression. Laughter therapy, anyone? I have seen a few articles on innovative laughter therapies that did not look bogus and claimed effectiveness. It could well be that scientists will end up laughing with them, rather than at them. Other, more serious experimental programs and interventions aimed at increasing human flourishing are being tried in developed countries.

At this juncture in global development, applied social science devoted to subjective well-being and happiness appears to be a worthy use of funding. Innovative programs should be encouraged as ecological and socioeconomic challenges increase and threaten the globe and our grandchildren's happiness. If, for instance, older, more materialistic perspectives on the pursuit of happiness overfocused on economic development and consumer consumption, then new research revealing that subjective human well-being correlates higher with inner and social variables should guide changes aimed at more qualitative, subjective goals. An overreliance on free-market forces to bring happiness may end up depleting natural, ecological, and social communal resources that actually produce higher levels of human happiness. "Excelsior!" may have to be retired as an inspiring poem and motto, along with remaining "über alles" rallying cries. Is it not possible, ask a growing number of social critics and government commissions, to run a society in ways that will increase subjective well-being as well as being green and sustainable? Such questions can arise in an era when increasing a nation's gross national happiness (GNH) is no longer dismissed as a Utopian goal. Highly respected new books on the politics of happiness are drawing on the emerging science of happiness to suggest innovative policies. When the respected former president of Harvard Derek Bok writes a book titled *The Politics of Happiness*, favorable to the new science of happiness, we know that it's an idea whose time has come. His wife, esteemed philosopher Sissela Bok, simultaneously published her book *Exploring Happiness: From Aristotle to Brain Science* with a fine discussion of the riches and ramification of the long-standing happiness quest. The larger cultural question may now be posed, "Why not now aim for a society where it is easy to be happy?" to paraphrase the words of activist Dorothy Day, who said she was working for a society where it is easy to be good. (Perhaps they are the same society?) In the even more immediate future, pressing questions arise focusing on the individual's pursuit of happiness.

The Individual and the Science of Happiness

Although all individuals, beginning in the womb, are formed and influenced by their family, cultural group, and ongoing social relationships, they also act to shape their environments and themselves. As the great social psychologist Kurt Lewin taught decades ago, individual human behavior and experience are functions of the individual person interacting with the environment; expressed mathematically the equation appears as $B = f(P, E)$. Untangling nature and nurture is never possible. Consequently it is worthwhile to study the characteristics, circumstances, and behaviors relevant to individual happiness. Who is happy and why? How does becoming happy happen? It must be more than luck or happenstance, as the etymology of the word "happy" might imply. There appear to be specific habits and attitudes present in persons that correlate with high scores on happiness measures, yet finding adequate ways to assess the inner subjective world of individuals is a perpetual problem.

Once more, familiar obstacles stand in the way. Happiness in individuals is an inner experience, and measurements include self-reports. To avoid errors, the timing, context, and cultural norms operating in any inquiry have to be taken into account. Think of the influence of social desirability pressures that operate in our upbeat, can-do American culture. A telling *New Yorker* cartoon appeared in the midst of the recent economic recession; it depicts two businessmen teetering on different window ledges of a skyscraper poised to jump. One man is saying to the other above him, "Oh, fine, thanks. And yourself?" Positive thinking and polite denial remain the order of the day. The corporate world that has been derided as irrationally brightsided is not alone; in many American circles the demand for false optimism makes it hard to find out how people feel. The answer is always, "Fine and dandy."

Since subjective consciousness and unhappiness can be hidden, suicides occur without warning. Outwardly functional persons reprise the ballad of Richard Corey. The enviably rich, handsome, and successful Richard Corey "went home and put a bullet through his head." With wealth and everything else to live for, why wasn't he happy? The worrisome question for psychologists faced with epidemics of youthful suicides is whether the Richard Coreys of the world can or will give accurate answers to questions about their subjective emotional well-being. This difficulty of tapping into individual consciousness has inspired a great deal of research ingenuity on the part of psychologists in depression and happiness research. In happiness research, direct questions and self-rating scales are supplemented by the use of peer observation, longitudinal measures, random experience sampling by iPhones, day reconstruction diaries, writing and drawing assignments, and other objective, nonobtrusive measures. Technological research tools continue to be devised, such as neuroimaging, physiological arousal measures, task response times, biochemical and genetic markers, microanalyses of facial videos, tracking eye movements, and an array of other measures that can be usefully combined. As it matures, psychological science advances in all of its experimental methodologies and complex tools of statistical analyses. Unfortunately, theoretical and intellectual consensus on the nature and potential of human beings is less advanced.

The new knowledge gained from genetics is also playing a big role in psychological investigations. Genetically inherited makeup is judged to be a factor in personality and temperamental differences, including happiness. Genes are a powerful determinant shaping individual bodies, brains, and behavioral responses to the environment. Recently, however, new puzzles have arisen in understanding the influence of genes on individuals—as in the discovery of mysterious genetic dark matter—which make scientists aware of how much more there is to understand. How do internal and external environmental factors affect gene expressions? Individual histories are shaped by genes as well as by environmental events, beginning in the womb. But however genes are turned on or off, it still seems true that genetic or epigenetic factors shape differences of temperament between individuals. Persons do not start on an equal playing field when it comes to happiness or personality. As a mother of many children, I could conclude by the time number five or six came along, "It's not really my fault that Sarah is irritable—or to my credit that David is one of those jolly, easy-to-rear babies."

In ancient times temperament was ascribed to the balance of humors circling in the body. To be more sanguine or bloody was good, but woe to those with too much black bile that produced melancholy. Today's research on individual differences has given up the typology of humors, but after decades of empirical testing has come up with the dimensional five-factor approach. People differ on the five factors of openness to experience, conscientiousness, extroversion, agreeableness, and neuroticism (or OCEAN). Naturally, agreeable extroverts (like the sanguine) can have a head start on happiness; from nursery school onward, extroverts excel in social intelligence and win the Best Camper awards. Remember as well, as a final proof positive, that in *Snow White and the Seven Dwarfs*, Grumpy could never be mistaken for Happy. Yet in the long run even Grumpy becomes happier after Snow White begins to love and care for them all. Each and every dwarf blooms and goes off each morning to whistle while they work. In Disneyland for sure, love and work triumph; grumps also can become happier ever after.

Researchers working on happiness inquiries find (to the surprise of many) that a majority of people say they are "moderately" happy. Unsurprisingly, those highest on subjective well-being measures have characteristics in common. A vast amount of collected data, including cross-cultural findings, shows that the happiest people are highly engaged in positive relationships with their families, friends, neighbors, and groups in their communities. They score high on optimism, self-esteem, resiliency, spirituality, and religious faith. Money appears to be of secondary importance, once there is enough to meet family needs and provide access to adequate rest and recreation. Happy individuals not only participate more in the lives of their families but also engage in more voluntary prosocial and altruistic helping behaviors in their communities. Work is also a source of satisfaction, and altruistic professions regularly produce the highest happiness scores. Whether formally religious or not, happy people report a high level of personal commitment to moral and spiritual values. Moreover, happy people do not seem to be self-consciously straining to become happy. One can wonder whether they read self-help books on happiness?

Indeed, a characteristic of happy people appears to be that they are directed outward toward relationships with other people and work; it makes sense that they should have less time or motivation to take their own emotional temperature. Nor would the happy tend to spend much time ruminating and letting their minds wander—another habit recently found to make individuals less happy. When asked, happy individuals can recognize that, yes, they are happy, and they express high levels of gratitude for their lives. Some thinkers have seen this perceived lack of attention to one's own happiness as a necessary condition for happiness; for them happiness can arrive only as a by-product, and a direct pursuit is bound to fail. But is this analysis nuanced enough?

Surely a self-conscious, rational person can observe her low or languishing levels of functioning and initiate efforts to improve. If you learn that certain actions make you happier, you can choose to pursue them directly, while avoiding those that are counterproductive. People can choose to take up exercise, meditation, prayer, listening to music, walking in the woods, visiting with friends, or helping in the local soup kitchen. When happiness follows, it can be greeted as a gift that I have made direct efforts to receive, not merely an unplanned by-product. Gardeners who want to enjoy flowers purposefully dig up the ground, plant seeds, water and weed, and appreciate the flowers that bloom as due to their efforts to receive the bounty of nature. Direct efforts to become happy can be similar to gardening. Individuals can profit from finding out which practices and psychological principles are helpful. Indeed, research psychologists are working to discover and disseminate reliable knowledge of the psychological ins and outs of happiness.

Using ingenious methods and tools, researchers have found that individuals often do not accurately predict their own future happiness—or lack thereof. As the investigators describe it, humans can be poor in "affective forecasting." Something that is foreseen as utterly unbearable (such as life in an iron lung) may in actuality not destroy all experiences of happiness. Conversely, an event that promises to bring immense happiness (such as winning a promotion or finally finishing your thesis) may not live up to expectations. Some great stroke of good luck or a finally achieved goal may only produce a temporary high because people do not foresee the new complications and problems involved.

Affective forecasting in the event of a setback or disaster can fail because people forget to take into account the future efforts they will make to cope and adapt. It may also be hard to forecast future emotional responses because of the way emotions exert powerful influences on thinking in general. Emotions have evolved to consist of vivid and moving responses to stimuli in order to further human survival. They can tend to sway or sweep thoughts in their wake, including projections for the future or memories of the past. In moments of despair I remember all my past failures; when angry at my boss (or spouse) I remember their long, long list of sins. One of the great advantages of feeling happy in the present is that it makes the future look bright and all projects doable. When happy or up, I'm energized or psyched and confident I can make things happen. If it doesn't work out, I'll just go on to the next best thing.

Time and future time are also theorized to play a role in pursuing happiness in another way, named the "hedonic treadmill" effect. The idea is that individuals adapt easily to present felt levels of happiness, so they inevitably and quickly become satiated and dissatisfied. When no longer happy in the present, individuals begin to seek new and increased sources of happiness. After adapting to the next increase, they again become dissatisfied—and an endlessly repeated run on the hedonic treadmill ensues. The fairy tale about the fisherman's wife and the magic fish who grants all wishes illustrates an insatiableness and escalation of desires for happiness. At first the wife desires only to have enough to eat, but soon she becomes dissatisfied and begins to up the ante. Step by step, she requests a house, then a palace, then goes on to demanding to be empress of all the world. (Or was it to be pope as well?) Only a final disaster stops her.

This cautionary folktale of humanity's insatiable desires for more and more glittering prizes and power exemplifies the treadmill effect. It voices a pessimistic view of humanity; we are so inherently, innately greedy that we can never achieve lasting happiness or be content. So since it is impossible, why try? At best, the ceaseless pursuit of ever greater and more happiness keeps the human species striving to reproduce and survive; at worst, the insatiable human desires for happiness bring more misery and environmental disaster in their wake.

Yet I am not convinced that the psychological treadmill effect actually applies beyond pathological cases of addictions—to drugs, alcohol, gambling, pornography, bulimia, self-cutting, and the like. Normal individuals self-regulate and return to healthy baselines. Granted, human beings adapt to conditions, or as the saying goes, "A man can get used to anything except hanging." And yes, it's true that the human brain seeks novel stimulation to function well. But needing new cognitive challenges in work and leisure activities may not apply to emotional happiness. In fact, a great deal of evidence exists, scientific and historical, that humans are attracted to the familiar. In experimental research, humans prefer familiar faces, landscapes, and objects over the unfamiliar. This innate positive attraction to well-known places, routines, and people is thought to have evolved because it helped early humans flourish. Bonding with mate, children, kin, tribe, and a home landscape energizes caretaking, defense, and group survival. Countless songs, poems, phrases, and stories describe the magnetic pull of home and family. "Home, sweet home," in my case it's a village on the banks of the lordly Hudson that makes my heartstrings zing. Familiarity does not breed contempt or even boredom. The joy of novelty can be found within familiar repeated cycles of work and celebration that mark the seasonal round. More to the point, happy people are found to be attached and engaged with their close families, friends, and local communities. They are not ceaselessly and restlessly striving for the new and best of everything. *Madame Bovary* or the *Sex and the City* crowd do not find the happy life.

Happiness and gratitude, like other positive emotions of joy, love, and interest move in upward spirals; positive emotions broaden interest and build new connections. I go to my friend's party, make more friends, and find out about a new volunteer opening. I go to the concert and end up joining the chorus. Each positive engagement builds more satisfaction and happiness. I then report more gratitude. Significantly, gratitude and thankfulness directly counter potential hedonic treadmills. Gratitude focuses on the good things in life happening here and now; it "accentuates the positive" and "eliminates the negative," as the lighthearted song has it. Feeling grateful is incompatible with envy, resentment, and anxious stress. It is surely no accident that in spiritual and secular interventions to increase happiness, the daily cultivation of gratitude is recommended. Different forms are practiced: meditation, gratitude lists, prayers of thanksgiving, gratitude letters, or telephone calls. In new psychological research, gratitude is described as serving "to find, remind, and bind people to caring individuals in their lives." These attitudes and practices are also described as instances of being mindful or focusing attention on the present.

But where does the scientific study of happiness end and prescribing and recommending practical applications begin? Science has traditionally required value-free objectivity and rejected bias or advocacy. Traditional spiritual and moral guidance accepts its advocacy role of mentoring and persuading, but does not lay claim to the authority of science or the scientific method. Can the science of happiness stay a science if and when it moves to self-help guidance and constructs steps and behavior you should follow if you want to find lasting happiness?

Are Applied Happiness Studies a Science?

When happiness studies move to intervention programs or psychological self-help recommendations, complicated questions rear up and critics weigh in. A therapeutic imperative recommending "Do this, do that, or avoid the other" is no longer a controlled scientific empirical study. Advice on how to generate positive emotions or how to adopt new thought patterns is not value-free or without bias. You leave standard scientific methods of discovery behind when you embark on giving directions on how to become happy. Scientific empirical investigations of correlations and causation are experimentally controlled investigations that require a disinterested third-party perspective. You adopt a persuasive advocacy stance when you aim to shape or induce people into valued new subjective experiences.

Consequently, the designation of science for such self-help and therapeutic interventions can be withheld or have its traditional academic boundaries stretched wide or blurred. The worst threat to academic respectability is to be labeled as indulging in junk science or pop pseudoscience. Bitter arguments over what is authentically science arise in fields dealing with subjective, conscious human beings. Psychology, anthropology, and sociology have had recent struggles between those who advocate traditional, objective, value-free scientific research, and those who practice subjectively interpretative and value-oriented approaches. Often looser scientific terms are adopted, such as "human science" or "interpretative science" or even calling an interpretative perspective "thick description." An applied "clinical" psychology has long faced ambiguity; is psychotherapy more of a persuasive educational art or is it a science?

One way to approach the applied interventionist efforts of happiness studies is to claim that they are scientific in their commitment to employing knowledge gained from rigorous scientific standards of research, but that they also go beyond this base in their openness to other forms of humanistic knowledge and value advocacy. When interventions are proposed on how to become happy, scientific information gained from academic research is used, but value-oriented moral virtues are advocated as well. Applied therapeutic or clinical efforts to help people in medicine, psychiatry, and psychology can hardly be value free; when the goal is to bring change for the better, the "better" must be identified and targeted at as a preferred value. Value-free empirical science can study what works in double-blind clinical trials, but not supply the moral goal or justification for change. Implicit or explicit value judgments govern what it means to become healthier, wiser, more virtuous, better functioning, or happier. Applied happiness interventions aimed at changing the lasting subjective experiences of an individual inevitably include implicit moral, philosophical, and religious value assumptions about what counts as a happy life. The scientific question, "What is the case?" or "What is the cause of this, and how does it operate?" can be addressed by strictly empirical and controlled methods of measurement. But this method is different from asking, "What counts as a desired, happy, and valuable outcome, and what must I as a specific individual do to become happy?"

A further complication in efforts to create a more valued subjective state such as individual happiness involves the individual's assent, consent, cooperation, and sustained efforts toward the goal. Self-conscious human beings can refuse, resist, or relapse. It is always simply assumed that every individual desires to be happy, but this assumption does not seem to take into account those who sabotage themselves. "Man can love his suffering," said Dostoevsky. A need for failure and love of suffering can be a perverse human reaction. Becoming happy can never be summarily and externally imposed without consent. For that matter, no one can become educated, moral, or good for another person.

In happiness—as in psychotherapy, education, moral formation, and religious conversion—individuals can, however, be guided, helped, and supported in the process of changing for the better. They can benefit from information, examples, collective experience, support, and scientific findings. Becoming happy, like becoming anything else, can make use of knowledge gathered by standard scientific research in human psychological operations. But applying scientific information appropriately presents other challenges. Science by its very nature can discover new information, often contradicting what went before. How are these ever-increasing, ad hoc research findings to be converted into stable practical guidance for unique individuals in varied circumstances? Group data in scientific results are averages and may not apply to a specific individual case. Directly opposite results may sometimes appear in research findings. One study may show that each additional child in a family diminishes happiness while a different article in the *Journal of Happiness Studies* reports a high positive correlation between the number of children a woman has and her happiness scores. (I like this study for personal reasons and because it goes against the prevailing wisdom.) But should either study be used in personal decision making? Such questions support the observation that pursuing and finding individual happiness is much more of an art than a science.

It is hard, for instance, to be convinced that everyone is equally poor at affective forecasting. Not many people are going to be condemned to life in an iron lung to find out. And if you are already an adult, it seems hardly possible to gain guidance from a study that finds that people are happier when they have grown up with a sister. Hard as experimenters try, disentangling cause and effect is difficult. Perhaps happy individuals are affected by some third or other preexisting variable. Averaged group data not only do not apply to individual cases, but they also can be outdated if conditions no longer prevail. When a nation, even in Scandinavia, suffers an economic crash or influx of immigrants, will it remain among the world's happiest places? It would certainly appear imprudent for a person to move to Denmark, or to Louisiana, in order to become happier. Taking the most sophisticated canonical scientific correlations and experiments on happiness and converting them into self-help guidance and programmed interventions can be a daunting venture.

Today the emerging school of positive psychology and its allies in happiness studies take on the above challenges with new strategies. Positive psychologists are among the leading advocates of using innovative scientific research to construct interventions to help people become happy. But at the same time they openly and innovatively incorporate traditional moral and humanistic values in their work. Could this be called a hybrid approach? The positive psychology movement maintains a scientific commitment to canonical, empirical scientific research on happiness and in psychology, while advocating virtue, discipline, and moral character as necessary for successful self-guidance programs. Their applied self-help programs may not actually count as basic or pure science, but they are scientific in their commitment to using information and principles gained from standard empirical research.

Positive psychology confidently affirms that human beings possess strengths and virtues that can be acquired, and this truth has too long been downplayed. Positive psychology wants to change and divert psychology's focus and overemphasis on human vulnerabilities, pathologies, and dysfunctions. It does not aim to supplant psychotherapies aimed at relieving the suffering of dysfunctions caused by posttraumatic stress syndrome, or abuse or violence or genetic causes; but positive psychology aims to supplement therapies by extending powerful new psychological strategies to better the human condition. Promoters of positive psychology contend that human beings have the capacity for intentionally generating emotional and intellectual change in themselves and thereby gaining lasting happiness. As with earlier humanistic psychologies there is a rejection of complete determinism. Positive psychology recognizes, however, that all are not equally able to achieve the same amount of happiness or human flourishing, but all may become happier. Individualizing the paths to happiness and selecting what works for an individual at his or her own level is part of the approach. This lesson is learned from the art of psychotherapy and the art of medicine. If many techniques are proved helpful it is advantageous to select those that work for the unique individual and that person's strengths.

Another feature of positive psychology that religious believers can welcome is its acceptance of spirituality and religious belief. Few in the movement appear to be religious themselves, but the claim is that when researching the history of human strengths and virtues it becomes undeniable that religious and spiritual resources are valuable and should not be excluded. Many persons are helped to become happy by spiritual and religious practices. Positive psychology is faith friendly in a way that older psychoanalytic and behaviorist orthodoxies never were. A few evolutionary scientists have also begun to see religious belief and practice as important in ensuring human survival and flourishing. While positive psychologists are faith friendly, the faith that receives the most favorable attention is the Zen Buddhism brought to America by the Dalai Lama. His Holiness and his Buddhist teaching emphasize the age-old ways to escape suffering and become happy; he has published a book titled *The Art of Happiness*. He also supports scientific psychology and sponsors collaborations and books with prominent American psychologists and neuroscientists. Buddhism backs up positive psychology's claims that human consciousness is central to reality and has the power to shape emotions and produce lasting happiness.

Buddhism proclaims a disciplined path to positive transformations of human beings; universal natural laws of upright right living and practices of meditation work. Other religious traditions of spiritual transformation, such as Christian spirituality, also exist in Western cultures, but appear less well known to positive psychologists. In their recommended self-help practices, individuals are simply told to practice a spiritual tradition, if you have one. A more necessary requirement in positive psychology's guidance is the practice of virtue and moral values. Their allegiance to Aristotle on virtue plays a central role. The necessity for virtue and a good life in order to obtain lasting and authentic happiness is clearly advocated. The adjectives "authentic," "lasting," or flourishing when applied to happiness serve to emphasize that positive psychology's goals are not to be confused with transitory superficial hedonism. Authentic happiness is more virtuous and stable than solely physically pleasant sensations or the granting of passing desires. Lasting happiness includes pleasure, but pleasures that, like emotions, are infused with personal meanings.

Admittedly, professional philosophical critiques of positive psychology's openness to morality and to spirituality could observe an amateur, slapdash quality. "What?" a philosopher was overheard to complain. "It's appalling that these psychologists think they can decide the nature of virtue and moral character by conducting an empirical poll of past cultures!" But compared to other psychologies where implicit assumptions and value perspectives are more or less smuggled in without a word, positive psychology can be credited for explicitly accepting and naming the moral values they advocate. Fortunately a lack of a highly developed, precise philosophical and metaphysical clarity does not keep a therapeutic intervention from effective results. It is progress that positive psychology is morally sensitive and faith friendly and believes that humans can change for the better.

Positive psychology also builds on the therapeutic techniques devised in cognitive and behavioral therapies that overcome resistance to change. Individuals can be helped by learning to apply psychological principles such as the power of habit, ritual, and reward conditioning. We all can learn to reward ourselves for making gradual progress toward goals. A cookie or candy kiss, perhaps? There are also powerful techniques used for changing appraisals and reappraisals to shape emotional responses. The strategies of cognitive reframing may be one of the best ways to pursue happiness because the inner voice of the self is always at hand. A cognitive reappraisal, for instance, such as, "He is in pain and really doesn't mean that insult," works. It can be combined with behavioral decisions to take a walk, clean the house, telephone a friend, listen to music, or pray for a sick community member. A person alerted to the power of imitation and habit formation can also consciously enact a desired emotion or action, until it becomes habitual. "Fake it until you make it," the AA mantra goes; "go and do likewise in imitation of

Christ," says the Christian. Practice your loving-kindness and letting-go meditations, says the Buddhist.

Other effective ways to change are for individuals to tap into the power of a chosen group's influence. Groups and networks shape us all the time, so we can learn to join up and make use of their power for a good end. Huge amounts of scientific research prove that birds of a feather flock together, and like it or not, you will be helped or hindered by social pressure. In its allegiance to scientific research to support self-help interventions, positive psychology votes for rationality. It is an exercise of prudence, to decide which evidence to selectively apply when, but it is far better than relying on vague, wishful thinking. A commitment to science differentiates positive psychology from popular self-help fads that overpromise and underperform. Invoking experimental findings as a primary authority also differentiates psychology from religious and moral paths of character education and formation, even though there is clearly a convergence between them. These convergences are explicitly acknowledged and valued by positive psychologists, although they are often criticized for stepping over the line by those demanding that science be value free.

Of course, historians of science can point to the fact that debates and conflicts always mark the ongoing course of science; fights become particularly bitter when new paradigms emerge and shifts of intellectual perspective in a culture emerge. Science is known as a cumulative enterprise of discovery in which new scientific findings may disprove, revise, or reconfigure established theories. In contrast, "Art is news that stays news," and philosophy and religion constantly tackle age-old questions and provide eternally examined answers. Ironically, science today may be experiencing what some scientists have called an impasse; the current state of ever-increasing, expanding scientific knowledge of the universe has produced an increasing sense of how much is yet unknown and hidden. Perhaps some paradigm shift will soon be on the horizon and bring more light. In the short run applied psychology's cooperation with moral and spiritual wisdom can be seen as a valuable move. Whom do you trust most, and must you even choose?

No jury has yet delivered a final verdict on the claim that scientific understanding and control of the subjective realm will always work to produce happiness. We seem only at the beginning of understanding human consciousness, human emotions, and human powers of will. But I am of the opinion that these innovative scientific efforts for becoming happy will be found to be valid, and usefully put into practice for the betterment of our human condition. My optimism is surely influenced by my Christian faith and my readings of other traditional sources of insight found in moral, artistic, and humanistic forms of knowledge. In support of my optimism I can cite other strands of scientific evidence that converge and strengthen the claim that, yes, humans can choose to change themselves for the better, and become happy—or happier.

Certainly, the science of happiness and the positive psychology movement did not like Athena spring forth fully formed from the brow of Zeus. Other discoveries in science during the last fifty years have made happiness studies possible—and credible. Before taking a brief glance at some of these key developments, I must declare a personal interest. My positive approach to happiness studies has evolved over four decades as a participant-observer in the crowded thickets of academic psychology, first as a graduate student, then as a tenured professor, and finally as a religious writer deeply committed to science, psychology, and theology.

Scientific Developments That Support Happiness Studies

In the last decades I have seen scientific theory and research take a decidedly positive turn. As all science has expanded, innovative scientific theories and research on evolution, emotion, cognition, consciousness, infant development, and brain studies have opened up new horizons for the study of human potential. In this new spaciousness, the emergence of a science of happiness has been able to find a place in the sun. Different scientific strands of evidence converge and give credibility to religious and philosophical claims that human beings can change, self-generate positive emotions, and become happier. Self-conscious agency with its powers of thinking is being reclaimed. "Man as the thinking reed" looks sturdier and "reasons of the heart" wiser, to crib from Pascal, a devout happiness pessimist who would be totally opposed to my arguments here. Just fifty years ago, elite academic psychology was dominated by a narrow mechanistic model of a human being; the reigning behaviorism concentrated experiments on conditioning stimuli and reflexes. Under the ideological dictates of this physical determinism, little attention was paid to self-consciousness, cognitive operations, the role of emotions, or the power of executive agency, popularly known to you and me as free will. Subjective consciousness was mostly off the radar screen of psychological scientific inquiry—as was altruism, moral development, religion, and artistic creativity. Today's well-known concepts of emotional intelligence and social intelligence were also waiting in the wings.

The two cultures of science and the humanities operated quite separately, as was thought right and proper. Real scientists relegated values and subjective conscious experiences to the vague and wooly realm of the humanities. Practitioners maintained clear boundaries between employing a third-person, scientific, objective approach and indulging in a first-person, subjectively emotional, and value-infused view of the world. An exception was made for clinical psychology, since it had to deal with real people's messy problems. But the pass that psychotherapy granted to subjectivity lowered psychotherapy's status in the academic pecking order. Who could possibly perform controlled experiments to find out what went on in therapy or whether it actually worked? Today's huge research enterprise devoted to validating different types of evidence-based psychotherapy was just beginning. Financial pressures from health insurance plans had also not yet appeared.

During this era, some alternative schools of humanistic psychology were on the scene, often in settings influenced by European, Jungian, or religious thought. Humanistic, existential, and gestalt schools of psychology often called themselves a third force in psychology, placed between the determinism of behaviorism and the determinism of the psychoanalytic Freudian establishment. Humanistic psychology continued affirming that self-conscious human persons freely act and change themselves to a large measure. Psychologists who stressed the processes of becoming self-realized were dedicated to helping people in value-oriented ways and so could be academically sidelined as soft and nonscientific. Meanwhile, followers of B. F. Skinner could boldly claim that scientific behaviorism had finally proved that humans were "beyond freedom and dignity," the title of Skinner's notorious book. For strict behaviorists, human consciousness was an irrelevant epiphenomenon, with no causal effect on human behavior or the environment. Human consciousness could only provide an illusion of free will. Such were the joys of the landscape of academic behaviorist psychology as it teetered on the brink of the intellectual eruption of the "cognitive revolution."

The field of psychology changed quite rapidly as a flood of new scientific knowledge poured forth. Ironically, the psychological study of cognition—the "mind's new science"—was stimulated by the development of artificial machine intelligence devised for computers. In addition, the advent of information theory and of communication science stimulated new psychological inquiries into human communication and cognition. Around the same period, innovative neuroimaging techniques were invented, and activity in the human brain could be visualized and correlated with subjective states of conscious experience. It became difficult to continue speaking of the brain as an irrelevant black box, as behaviorists were wont to do. Empirical images of an active, conscious brain/mind revived older views that had persisted in common sense and folk psychology—that human thinking could cause human behavior and exert causal control of internal and external environments. Funding for research on cognition became available, and soon cognition became a subspecialty of psychology.

Cognitive science engaged in explorations of the contents, patterns, differing frameworks, and causal outcomes of thinking. For human beings, the cognitive appraisal and interpretation of the meaning of an event shaped the response. Consequently the cognitive revolution quickly generated cognitive therapies focusing on changing a person's maladapted thinking that furthered problems such as depression. Inner thoughts—such as "Everyone always hates me, and I always fail at everything"—were challenged. When cognitive therapies and behaviorist therapies joined techniques—incorporating cognitive methods and behaviorist methods of conditioning—strategies became available for positive psychology's interventions aimed at happiness.

Almost simultaneously, new discoveries of the innate capacities of infant intelligence were studied. The infancy barrier to research was overcome by ingenious new nonverbal techniques involving eye gaze, facial expressions, smiles, and other nonverbal responses of infants. A delightful experiment featured researchers rewarding infants by popping into view and giving forth a cheery "peek-a-boo." Studies of infant language acquisition and human intelligence contributed depth and breadth to the cognitive revolution. The groundbreaking work of the great Piaget on the development of children's intelligence was at last given its due—even if he had been an unorthodox scientist and first observed his own children outside of any laboratory. Piaget inspired research on cognition and the unique mental powers of human beings. That human beings were significantly different than pigeons and rats became undeniable.

When subjective consciousness and thinking became approved objects of scientific psychological investigations, further developments rapidly took place. Certain elements of conscious thinking are infused with a qualitative immediacy and vividness that signal personally invested meanings and relevance. These could be called "hot cognitions" because of their personal vibrancy, and they are now recognized as subjective emotional responses. Emotions are described in every language. Philosophers had named such responses as "qualia," for the nonverbal qualitative sense of the feelings. In rapid fashion, psychologists began to identify, classify, and study human emotions as subjective responses and to recognize their central importance in human functioning. Another emerging subspecialty in psychology sprang up: the psychology of emotion, complete with its own journals, specialists, and research projects. The questions to be explored include: What are emotions? Where do they come from? How do they operate and interact with human thinking, behavior, physiology, and other emotions? I call this movement the "emotion explosion" that followed on the cognitive revolution.

At this auspicious juncture on the brink of new and exciting times in psychology I entered a PhD program in social and personality psychology. I came as a former English major and enthusiastic student of theology eager to explore science. Right before these new movements had fully arrived, I had proposed an MA thesis on the role of appraisal in emotions. This being the late 1970s, before the new developments had become established, I was tactfully informed that neither emotions nor cognitive appraisals were significant enough topics on which to waste research time. Subjective consciousness and cognition were still thought to be so irrelevant that one psychologist of the period maintained that sleep (not dreams) could be considered an emotion, given that emotions were nothing but physiological responses.

Fortunately I completed my master's thesis anyway and entered a PhD program in time for interest in subjective consciousness to become scientifically acceptable. Studies of the self were increasing, and subjective thinking and emotion were embraced as vital topics. Admittedly one of my professors operationally defined the self to be "person A as observed by person A," but he was still opening up new directions of research. Eventually I completed my experimental doctoral dissertation, "Self-Consciousness and Promises"—a topic as distant from the observations of pigeons and rats as you could get, but how satisfying for a former English major and future writer on topics of theological and moral development.

The passing decades have brought more rapid expansion and breadth to psychology, producing a rich, varied, and challenging scientific field that moves forward, inward, upward, and outward, with more and more interdisciplinary projects. Psychology has returned to the broader, more comprehensive explorations of its nineteenth-century founding genius William James (my personal hero). At last the gibe that "psychology has lost its mind" or suffers from a bad case of "physics envy" no longer applies. By its very appearance the emerging science of happiness is evidence of the change in the weather that has taken place. Psychological studies of self, thinking, consciousness, and emotion are accorded scientific respectability; research is taking place not only on happiness but also on self-consciousness, moral development, religious belief, aesthetic creativity, and a host of other uniquely human capacities. Moreover, in the usual pattern of quickly incorporating research into clinical applications and interventions, there now exist happiness interventions that join with cognitive therapies, emotion- and affect-based therapies, behavioral therapies, cognitive-behavior therapies, interpersonal therapies, and psychoanalytic therapies, along with others too numerous to name. In all its thousands of flowers blooming, present psychology includes the recognition that thinking, behavior, and emotions constantly interact and produce potentials for individual change. The ground for scientific happiness studies has been surveyed, plowed, and seeded, and now the crop is ready to be consumed. The taboo topics of subjectivity and consciousness have already been allowed into the tent. Happiness is, after all, subjective, self-conscious, emotional, pleasurable, and influenced by moral appraisals and evaluations.

Yet scientific happiness studies might never have been conceived or sustained without the triumph of Darwin's great idea. Evolutionary thought, research, and theory have themselves been evolving since Darwin's big bang in the nineteenth century, but by now evolutionary theory exerts a powerful influence over a host of intellectual and scientific fields—including happiness studies. Evolutionary understandings of human origins have been particularly influential in psychology, anthropology, psychiatry, and neurology. What is now called evolutionary psychology, another subspecialty, emerged from its first incarnation in sociobiology. Evolutionary science now shapes studies of human cognition, emotion, sexuality, morality, infancy, linguistics, religion, art, music, and group dynamics—to name a few.

Evolutionary theory supports the advent and credibility of happiness studies and interventions in critical ways. First is the clear message that, in our universe, dynamic change over time is the essential characteristic of life, even in the origin of the human species. More specifically, evolutionary research and theory have shown the importance of human emotions and the adapted nonconscious mind in ensuring human survival. Most recently, positive emotions have received due credit in effectively furthering the evolution of humankind. Emotions are no longer thought to be peripheral or unnecessary in survival. Happiness and subjective well-being have moved to center stage and are recognized as valuable and unique resources of Homo sapiens.

Equally important for happiness studies is the evolutionary support for claims that human organisms are equipped to self-generate change in thinking and emotions. The slow evolution of the human brain and body has resulted in a whole organism made up of a multitude of interacting modular subsystems; they work separately and cooperatively to give human beings flexibility and adaptability. One system can influence another to better ensure functioning and survival. The gradual evolutionary expansion of the brain, with its complex levels of cognitive functioning, has produced different levels of operating intelligences and different kinds of consciousness that cooperate and mutually influence each other.

Moreover, evolutionary selection means that humans are not born as blank slates, but rather come into the world equipped with innate, pan-specific capacities and predispositions. Every baby has a head start in the human race. The species possesses a psychic unity with essential core characteristics that local variation may only moderately modify. Cultures all have far more in common than not; happiness and joy, like all the primary emotions, are universal response systems.

It seems pretty clear, however, that from birth, and before, innately programmed systems develop and become more organized and integrated into adulthood. But after the age of reproduction has passed, human organisms are subject to the material laws of biological life; they begin to deteriorate, disintegrate, and eventually physically die. But humans possess a unique factor that is still mysterious: their capacity for physical brains to produce consciousness and self-consciousness. Experientially in daily life, firsthand self-consciousness is the thing we know most intimately, yet understand the least. Experiences of happiness participate in this reality of subjective consciousness. Whence comes the sense of self and the self-conscious I that can direct and influence all the other systems while being necessarily and simultaneously supported, influenced, facilitated, and constrained by them? And where do inner conflicts come from? The pursuit of subjective well-being and happiness become caught up in these unique human problems and potentialities.

With the development of language, humans can think in abstract ways as no other animal can. Rational selves or minds can imagine the future and think of how things could be different than they are now—such as being happier. Things not immediately perceived in space or time can be envisioned or remembered—like a dead mother's love or my own future death. More prosaic futures probably are more often the object of conscious attention, like preparations for the next meal or a coming holiday weekend. Thinkers equipped with different kinds and levels of conscious capacities, including emotional motivations, can initiate, plan, and solve difficult problems in the present or coming week. With these abilities I can plan to act, including pursuing happiness. Because of the different flexible systems at the ready, I can pursue a goal and entrain other operating systems to carry it out. When I initiate a goal my muscles move, perceptual and emotional responses are activated, intuitions and memories are called into play, and attention is sustained. In other words, evolved humans beings are known to have evolved the capacity to imagine, desire, intuit, deliberate, choose, and move toward a goal with many automatic actions. Without this evolutionary history, humans would not have survived.

While the conscious I and self can deliberately initiate action, different nonconscious operating systems perform a lot of human heavy lifting without awareness or planned effort. This advantage is huge, since rational conscious thinking takes time and energy and is slow. It is most efficiently saved for new and difficult problems or projects. What if we had to consciously direct our liver, heartbeat, lungs, or immune system every minute of the day? The calculations required for muscle movements or perception would leave us paralyzed. Thank God that millions of years of evolutionary selection have produced automatic adaptive functioning systems that keep us alive and let us have the freedom to use and enjoy self-consciousness. The conscious I can be alerted when needed, as in a new challenge or conflict, and can be free to initiate creative and artistic projects. Automatic mindlessness makes voluntary attentive mindfulness possible, and both play a part in happiness and other emotions. The self-conscious I is like a pilot flying a highly computerized jet plane; the pilot hardly notices the ongoing smooth functioning of the plane, but at decisive moments, or when some emergency arises, the pilot must become alert and act. Perhaps even then, pilots save themselves and their passengers through the spontaneously adaptive intelligent responses that operate instantly.

Exciting new psychological research is focusing today on our evolved, adaptive, nonconscious minds. If the adaptive nonconscious knows more than logical reason knows, or at least knows it faster, how do the two operating systems work together? And to what effect? The nonconscious system is thought to have evolved earlier, and so is faster, more emotional, and more global than precise or logical. Intuitions that are more emotional arise from these adaptive processes, as in our hunches or gut feelings. Since these feelings are the legacy of millions of years of evolutionary adaptation of the evolving brain/mind, they can sometimes provide accurate signals and reactions that help solve problems, and they have a role in our gaining happiness as well. Our minds can be processing more cues and signals than we consciously notice, and they may be helping us in decisions, discoveries, and insights. Malcolm Gladwell has popularized these capacities in the book *Blink*.

But unfortunately, intuitions and hunches can also be wrong. Haven't we all had intuitions that were dead wrong as well as those that were right on target? Perhaps we possess nonconscious responses from our deep evolutionary past or early childhood learning that don't apply to present reality. Racial stereotypes and other nonconscious perceptions may not only be inapplicable but can be incompatible with our rational, moral, and religious commitments. Unrealistic and neurotic fears, phobias, and other maladapted reactions can be nonconsciously triggered. Mistaken drives for false happiness may exist along with poor affective forecasting. The possibility of errors in the nonconscious adaptive system may be the price humans pay for its advantages in functioning.

Emotions too are often nonconsciously stimulated and arrive much like intuitions. **We** have whole, full-bodied organic emotional responses tapping into deeper streams of experience than logical abstract thought. We are not computers or machines. We need our emotional hot cognitions, our qualia, or our spontaneous, gut-intuitive responses to be fully human. Subjective, emotional feelings and mysterious qualitative responses that infuse consciousness are centrally important to human happiness. No abstract syllogism, logical argument, or algorithm by itself can produce subjective, qualitative feelings of happiness; they are received as whole-bodied gifts because they arrive from sources below awareness.

All those in a how-to-become-happy enterprise—whether spiritual, moral, or psychological—have to address the issue of how humans can integrate all their evolved human systems into a harmonious, well-functioning whole. While humans need their spontaneous emotional responses and intuitions, including warnings and inspirations, they must not slight the self-conscious I's rational ability to initiate, direct, criticize, monitor, correct, and suppress or inhibit responses. Say yes, yes, but be able to say no.

Happy people seem to achieve a balance of spontaneity and self-monitoring. Creative artists are inspired by their nonconscious, spontaneous flowing of emotional responses (the muses of antiquity?) and also engage in hypercritical analysis and revisions. In science also, the game is to guess well, then test well. Who has the most creative hypothesis and then tests it most rigorously? Critiquing and checking intuitions and emotional impulses through critical reasoning is the essence of prudence, but letting emotions have their innings may also be important and beneficial. William James well understood that human consciousness had different levels and operations; he advised that the art of successful living (including happiness?) lay in acknowledging, using, and cultivating the resources and powers of one's nonconscious, intuitive mind in interaction with the highest powers of self-conscious rationality. Also, because every individual is unique, each has to find her or his individual path through the common human landscape.

At this point, scientific psychology's study of consciousness has not caught up to the philosophical insights in James's science and psychology. James was sure that we live in a pluralistic, open, undetermined universe, where enough openness and chance could give humans freedom to choose and to act. The open future was determined by human action, and chance operated to confer freedom to human beings. Not only can humans choose, they can continue to persevere in their chosen efforts. James speaks of the "mysterious" human power of "resolve." In ordinary language we talk about willpower and assume that we all have free will. Such assertions of freedom to choose and to change ourselves are concepts still avoided in scientific psychology, where the legacy of determined worldviews still lingers in the air. Slowly, however, as scientific investigations increasingly turn to self-control and emotion regulation, the concept of a self-conscious, intentionally acting I seems to be slipping back into the conversations. In some research it is just assumed, and in other studies we read of "executive functioning," "attention deployment," "cognitive effortful control," "overriding top-down control," "reappraising and reframing," or "modulating," "downgrading," "upregulating," and "amplifying."

At times the older Freudian term of "ego" or "I" is revived to describe the acting executive. The ego, like the will, can wax and wane in strength and energy. Intriguing new theories appear of the way prolonged, effortful, controlled concentration on a task depletes the ego. When ego depletion sets in, further efficient functioning is impaired, and the capacity to concentrate and resist temptations and distractions wanes. This idea of ego depletion hits home with me, and I predict a great future for its use. "Weakness of will" has been a perennial philosophical problem, but new psychological inquiry may address it again. Psychological research shows that ego depletion arises from personal losses, setbacks, and negative emotions, in addition to fatigue. Loss of emotional regulation and lessened resistance to temptation arise from ego depletion—no surprise there. Think of AA's cautions against hunger, loneliness, anger, and fatigue. Yet significantly, positive emotions like joy and interest are found to replenish the depleted ego, and enhance self-regulation. Enhancing self-control through positive emotions is a very important research finding that confirms the importance of happiness studies and throws more light on the evolution and operation of human emotions.

When evolutionary psychology first emerged, the main focus was on the negative emotions that facilitated defensive and aggressive responses. Fear and anger, fight or flight, were seen as important for motivating competitive and aggressive behavior that would ensure survival. Self-interested dominance and aggressive control of resources furthered success in mating and reproduction. Since humans depend upon social groups for protection and provisioning, individuals must conform to the group or perish. Guilt, shame, sorrow, contempt, and disgust are pan-specific, and negative secondary social emotions that reinforce group norms.

Negative emotions that serve self-interest and defense were useful to the evolutionary process insofar as they allowed more of an individual's genes to pass into the next generation. Deception and self-deception were also thought to be built-in, inherited predispositions that served mating success and the acquisition of social status. If you could manage to hold back or hide a larger share of the spoils of the hunt for yourself, you profited. If you deceived yourself that your grabbing power was altruistically motivated for the common good, you could more whole-heartedly exploit others.

But the positive emotions that Darwin recognized were less noted at first because they were more difficult to explain. As the question was phrased, "What are positive emotions for?" The core positive emotions are usually differentiated as joy, interest, love, and contentment. More complex secondary positive emotions, such as pride, are sometimes included along with other mixtures. Why have I always loved receiving gold stars, and what could be more rewarding than hearing words of praise? Still, how do these positive emotions help anyone to survive?

Psychologists studying the topic have found that, in general, emotions are important to survival because they serve to instantly communicate information about the external or internal environment to others, and to oneself. Basic emotions can be universally identified and communicated because they are expressed with specific patterns of facial expressions, physiological reactions, postures, appropriate conscious experiences, and motivational action tendencies. We innately read these messages. They may be triggered instantaneously, and normal humans can recognize and decode them quickly, beginning in infancy. Positive emotions motivate humans to approach or continue; negative emotions motivate humans to avoid, avert, or correct.

Within the ongoing stream of waking consciousness, different emotions emerge with different patterns and degrees of intensity; they also fade and recede in characteristic patterns. Negative emotions can quickly and dramatically mobilize individuals to defensive actions in order to cope with danger and adverse situations. When a tiger approaches or a fire breaks out, get moving. In contrast, positive emotions, such as happiness, move individuals to continue, approach, or savor safe and favorable conditions or activity. I am where I want to be, or I am doing what I want to be doing. With humans, the appraisals or meanings of events determine which emotions arise. We subsequently learn associated cues as well. The stream of consciousness during waking activity can include the rise and fall of thoughts and emotions in such complex patterns that musical analogies are most useful for describing the process: recurrent themes, chords, fugues, harmonies, and dissonance, for example. Of course, other art forms can also convey and reproduce positive emotional experience and personal meaning: color, tempo, warmth, and energy.

But positive emotions such as joy, interest, and love are today recognized as contributing to human survival in generating affective bonding, cooperation, altruism, mating, parental nurture, and kinship care. Without positive, altruistic nurturing, infants die, and you don't get your genes into a surviving generation. If you don't produce altruistic adult children, no grandchildren survive. Human attachments of love and interest ensure altruistic nurturing, sharing, provisioning of scarce resources, cooperative work, and defense against predators. The positive emotions of joy, interest, and love create the motivating desires to mate and survive. Positive emotions also motivate the joyful and interesting celebrations, art, and rituals that make life worth living. A good case can be made that human survival depends mainly on positive emotions and happiness. Negative emotions narrow attention and can aid in defense and social conformity, but they can also depress drives for provisioning, nurturing, and reproducing. Hate, anger, and aggressive warfare can even lead to physical extinction of warring human groups. In contrast, positive emotions engender and energize family life, friendship, sex, work, play, art, music, dance, religion, morality, healing, and cooperative community morale.

The most recent research on positive emotions of love, joy, and interest has discovered that they are potent means for healing individual traumas and undoing memory's psychic wounds. Successful therapeutic work with victims of abuse and torture are examples of these powerful healing forces. As previously noted positive emotions encourage continued engagement with others in positive upward spirals and broaden and build skills by accruing valuable information. In happy states, individuals are found to be more creative and effective in problem solving. When you are happy, you feel safe and are free to be more playful and experimental.

The core positive emotion of interest should never be overlooked. It engenders discoveries as well as problem solving. Could human invention and technological progress in human history have happened without positive emotions of interest? Interest initiates projects but also motivates perseverance in problem solving; there is the wonderful moment when we finally arrive at the solution and an aha experience. "The rain in Spain stays mainly on the plain," pronounces Eliza after days of effort. "By George, she's got it," and a celebration erupts.

The positive emotion of interest and engagement is now famously called flow, a source of satisfaction and happiness. As demonstrated in child's play, or a rock climber's ascent, flow produces pleasure in the process as much as the goal, and results in an expanded sense of self. Happiness arrives in flow experiences when the task is absorbing and neither too difficult nor too easy, but like Baby Bear's porridge, just right. In addition to studies of flow, other research finds that persons are happier when their attention is focused. Fortunately, focus—and happiness—can occur in many ways.

An innovative technique of random experience sampling using programmed cell phone devices collected data on individual happiness at different times of the day and night. The highest happiness ratings were reported during sexual activity. And why not? Sex can have everything: the focused attention of flow; an engrossing, interpersonal relationship building up bonding; and intensely pleasurable physical and physiological responses. One of those physiological responses during sex is the release of the peptide oxytocin, which nursing mothers also produce to calming, happy, and trusting effect.

Another innovative research contribution toward reappraising the role of positive emotions has been the study of altruism and brain imagery. Individual acts of altruism and giving to others trigger reward responses in the brain that correlate with positive subjective feelings. To give is to get, these experiments show. This initial new finding has been labeled as an instance of the helper principle, which serves to explain why humans feel so good and happy when they choose to give things to others. If altruism is shown as an innate human predisposition that human beings evolutionarily selected, then another one-sided negative view of human nature is invalidated.

Inspired by positive psychology, other researchers have added to the positive reappraisals of human nature and the credibility of happiness studies. Human strengths, virtues, and positive emotional characteristics are receiving scientific empirical support. New research studies have been investigating human predispositions and capacities for forgiveness, peacemaking, morality, religious belief, gratitude, humility, empathy, compassion, hope, humor, creativity, flow, and self-efficacy. These standard scientific researches are available in a recently published *Handbook of Positive Psychology*, as well as in many other academic journals. If you want to see how science has taken a positive turn, these sources are a good start.

Even more recent and extremely positive research supports humans' pro-social nature. Scientific discovery and attention has focused on the automatic capacity of humans to respond to others with empathy. Empathy is defined as the spontaneous response of an observer who directly experiences and re-creates the feelings and response of the one who is observed: "I feel what you are feeling and can read your mind because my brain is automatically responding as yours is." These spontaneous responses of empathy appear to be the work of newly discovered and as yet mysterious mirror neurons in the organism. Are they only in the brain, or elsewhere? While much remains unknown, research appears to show that such mirroring systems produce the all-important innate human capacity to empathize, to imitate, and to read the minds of others.

Human empathy that works to shape thinking and feeling may be the power that makes humans measurably different from all other forms of life. It can't help but be an exciting development. We have all felt that oneness, that union of mind and heart with another—flesh of my flesh, bone of my bone, heart of my heart. Poets have expressed this kind of love and union. Mothers and babies commune in empathy, eye gaze, and other mutually shared feelings. In psychotherapy research, the main source of the healing power has been seen as the mutual shared consciousness of empathy between client and therapist that takes place in the present moment. This empathy and oneness of consciousness can give great happiness; our hearts burn within us. When we finally discover more about mirror neurons, we may come closer to better understanding emotions, empathy, shared consciousness, and the happiness that is beyond words.

Certainly, infancy studies are moving toward new understandings of interpersonal, preverbal communications of loving oneness that have beneficial effects. Beginning in infancy, humans have the capacity to read the emotions and motivations of others in their environment—if they are not impaired in some unfortunate way by autism or brain damage. Infants don't have verbal speech, but they are now considered to have stunning capacities to create meaning in their life with others. For a hypersocial species, no capacity is more important for human flourishing than communicating with others. If this capacity of empathetic mind reading is absent or skewed, then emotional reactions and social functioning will be seriously skewed as well. Social intelligence seems rooted in the earliest mother-child dance of emotions.

The presence and functioning of empathy explain how emotional responses like happiness are instantly contagious. When you laugh, I laugh; when you weep, I weep, even without knowing why. Happiness and joy are infectious and energize as they delight. Happiness can increase through nonconscious processes that increase intimate bonding without words. Self-other sharings of consciousness continue throughout life and seem particularly powerful in families, friendship, healing, celebrations, and worship.

Just as important, spontaneous empathy may be the source of the innate moral senses that psychologists are now finding in new research. Empathy can develop into more cognitively shaped and complex responses of sympathy. In sympathy I can cognitively understand that you are different from me, even as I empathize and feel one with you. I can sense your feelings but also know that your needs may be different from mine. Toddlers may bring a weeping adult their own bottle or blanket for comfort, while an adult would be more discriminating in offers of sympathy and help. Innate spontaneous empathy and sympathy motivate helping but also generate moral feelings and actions. Altruistic acts may be initiated by empathetic responses that are translated into action—often instantaneously and nonconsciously. Empathy, sympathy, and altruistic responses produce the building blocks for the moral commitments to justice, fairness, and peacemaking that are so crucial for collective and individual happiness. Again, such positive moral responses appear to emerge surprisingly early, as the increasing research in infant and child psychology attests. Many researchers are now finding, unexpectedly, that babies not only can respond with empathy to others, they can read their intentions and have innately intuitive moral perceptions of others. Popular articles on the moral baby complement more academic books on the philosophical baby. The moral sense that is developed so early in association with emotions may explain how happiness can gain the moral quality of goodness and worthwhileness. The good feeling and the valued good are united from the beginning. Happiness is known as a worthwhile good before it can be expressed verbally or logically reasoned. Take that, Aristotle; you just didn't know about the philosophical baby with moral perceptions and meaning-making abilities. To be fair, neither did William James.

Infants are viewed as born for happiness because they are innately delighted and enthusiastic learners. They come equipped and ready to feel the positive emotions of interest, joy, and love. Babies also find happiness in focused engagement and exploration of their novel environment. After all, everything is new to them. The present moment is the concentrated center of existence, and like Adam and Eve, "The world lies new before them." This active, open engagement of babies is described as one of "lanternlike happiness." It has also been compared to the meditative states of consciousness that adults can achieve when they mindfully focus attention and stay in the present moment. Buddhists claim that this disciplined consciousness is the way to happiness. Of course, babies who are nurtured and cared for also have the physiological joys of nursing, touching, smelling, and intimate eye gaze and smiling to further their happiness. In babies, as in the happiest of adults, the positive emotions of interest, joy, love, learning, and play become intertwined in contagious gladness. Child psychologists have described the child's "love affair with the world." No wonder anthropologists find that the babies of the tribe are the center of attention and laughter. Even in the developed world, babies can magnetically attract positive attention and bask in positive emotions; they are like fires on the hearth providing warmth and delight. The Romantic poets correctly paid homage to the innate positive qualities of infant happiness when describing them coming into the world "trailing clouds of glory." Optimists can take heart and see convincing evidence that innate positive emotions of joy, interest, and mutual love light up human life early and late.

Of course, realistically, it has to be admitted that huge amounts of suffering, darkness, and gloom exist in the world, another specialty of the Romantic poets. Babies cry and can have miserable periods, even if they are not neglected, abused, or suffering skewed parenting.

Granted, too, that many natural and socially created obstacles to human happiness exist. The problem of why evil and suffering exist in life is a question that can cloud the emerging science of happiness. But already overwhelming attention has been paid to suffering, to the forces of evil, and to the destructive devices and desires of the human heart. Despite all of these sad truths, the pursuit of happiness has never been given up, and the emerging science of happiness can help explain why. It adds to the assurance of traditional wisdom that suffering need not triumph. Yes, sorrows come; in particular, empathy with the suffering of others is part of a good life lived in loving relationship with others. But here, too, positive emotional resources exist.

One critical point about the evolution of emotions and happiness can be repeated. In evolutionary development humans have acquired many multilevel and modular functioning systems. Since the positive emotional system and the negative emotional system are seen as structurally different and independent they can be independently activated; they can be simultaneously activated. The positive emotional systems of joy, interest, love, and contentment are real and not to be simply defined as nothing but relief from suffering (as some pessimists have held). Nor, as some poets would have it, must suffering be a facet of happiness, as in "your sorrow is your joy," or vice versa. Independence of systems also will discount the claim of some moralists and Romantics that suffering is the necessary precursor of joy. Happiness and positive pro-social emotional responses can exist without first paying the price of pain. Joy, love, empathy, bonding, morality, and altruism are primary human capacities, not just secondary reactions or defenses. If negative emotions can be seen as playing a role in signaling danger and motivating avoidance and correction, they cannot permanently eradicate the positive emotions intrinsic to human nature.

Joy and suffering, as independent emotional systems, can, however, be activated at the same time. Any innocent or altruistic suffering in empathy with another, or even within oneself, need not suppress the possibility of happiness. In other words, happiness need not be dependent upon detaching and separating from others in their pain. Positive emotions of love, altruism, and happiness can be felt along with empathetic suffering with others, sometimes called "compassion." Positive and negative emotions can also alternate in quicksilver streams of shifting consciousness. These complex experiences of subjective consciousness can explain the nuance and subtlety of times in which joy and sorrow, or rewarding satisfactions and suffering, can quickly alternate or coexist. A mother can be joyfully and agonizingly giving birth, or a father can joyfully and painfully be rescuing his son from a fire. In experimental research, grieving widows have reported the simultaneous emotions of mourning and happiness as they rejoice in the love felt in their marriage while mourning its loss. In other, more extraordinary coexisting emotional states, exalted ecstatic martyrs have rejoiced in the midst of their agonizing pain and suffering. Their deepest altruistic commitments and triumphant emotions could accompany the torture.

In ordinary, everyday lives, a person's deeper, more central, and stable core emotions of happiness and love can also coexist with passing sufferings and sorrow. I can be deeply and lastingly happy and yet experience negative superficial emotions that are unimportant and which pass quickly without destroying my underlying stability. Since emotions have been seen as evolving to bring us tacit information about the inner and external environment, certain negative emotions can signal or inform me of something I need to know. Some corrective move may be needed. A deeply happy person need not become impervious to negative signals or the sufferings of others in the world in order to be happy. When it is recognized that joy can coexist with negative emotions, even costly altruism need not be shunned.

Empathetic suffering in particular is accompanied by the growth of positive emotional feelings of nurturing love and engagement. The enlarging of the self through giving and sharing can strengthen the happiness that comes from giving. Intersubjective consciousness can be engendered that not only heals but brings its own reward. Blessed are those who mourn. When suffering with others—or better, for others—the bonding and the altruism can be intrinsically rewarding and satisfying.

It would seem difficult, if not impossible, to be happy while simultaneously driven by hate, envy, vengefulness, fear, greed, lust, or guilty shame. When negative emotions are causing harm to self or others, they can hardly feel worthwhile and positive. Negative emotions rarely benefit others or enlarge the self by moving toward others. The self-focused agitation of unfulfilled desire is so painful that few would count it as enlarging the self or able to coexist with happiness. No one can positively savor or hope that consuming selfishness should continue. The operations of the emotional system seem to contribute to two morally relevant conclusions: to pursue happiness and become happy does not imply adopting a self-protective disregard of others, and the advent of non-blameworthy suffering does not make happiness impossible. To pursue happiness is a good and worthy goal with many benefits to self, others, and the world at large. And it is possible to succeed.

The I, Self, or executive function that pursues happiness must be able to regulate and shape the innate human capacities of thinking and emotions. But an older ideal of dominating the lower animalistic body and emotions no longer fits the evolutionary story. A "higher" rational soul does not achieve self-regulation simply by dominating, suppressing, or detaching from the "lower" irrational, physical, and emotional functions of the human being. Today the mind-body-brain-spirit unity is recognized as a whole interacting system comprising vitally necessary conscious and nonconscious subsystems. The human organism is the product of millions of years of evolutionary adaptive learning, and possesses many complex resources for carrying out beneficial actions in the environment. Self-consciousness and highly logical and rational thinking will welcome and employ every resource in the game.

New evidence for voluntarily and successfully pursuing happiness can be found in new psychological specialties devoted to self-control and emotion regulation. As emotions have become a dominant interest in psychology and neuropsychology, attention turns to emotion regulation. The complex processes involved are directly related to overcoming obstacles to becoming happy and sustaining happiness. Emotional intelligence is described as including the ability to recognize emotions in self and others and to successfully regulate them appropriately. Individual regulation of emotion consists of the ability to dampen, redirect, or amplify the spontaneous emotional responses. Since emotions emerge in ongoing time in response to events in the inner and external environments, they can be shaped or modulated at different points in the process, with different strategies deployed. I can recognize that a personally unacceptable emotion, like envious resentment, is rising up within, and nip it in the bud by strategic interventions. Some familiar cognitive and behavioral strategies already noted employ exercise, food, hot water, nature walks, and other physical pleasures; others employ social, intellectual, artistic, and spiritual activities. Music and movies may have particular powers to distract and regulate emotions. Go to spiritual masterpieces for a full array of positive human resources for becoming happy. Science and therapy are almost drawing even.

Persons change their emotions by voluntary acts of resolve, willpower, and imagination. Those more adept at emotion regulation are more happy and well functioning, as recent research unsurprisingly shows. Sometimes the skills of self-regulation have been so thoroughly learned in earlier socialization in the family and cultural group that they become as automatic and unconscious as riding a bike. A familiar psychological pattern is seen in which an effortful conscious action, such as learning to drive, gradually becomes automatic. This may be the explanation of why truly virtuous, good, and holy persons can be so natural and humble: they have become so emotionally integrated with their standards of valued behavior that they don't need or notice conscious efforts to emotionally regulate their responses. They may get the emotional signal and cue instantly, but just as instantly and spontaneously react positively.

Infants and small children can, from an early age, be observed learning and practicing emotional self-regulation. Infants look away or suck their thumbs to soothe themselves. Children also quickly learn family and cultural norms for emotional display rules. In modern Western societies, we don't laugh at funerals or tear our hair out or jump into graves howling with grief. When infants and children fail in their progress toward emotional regulation, the results are evident: tantrums, aggression, and sobbing collapse into sleep. In adults these lapses have been described as "emotional wildfires," "emotional flooding," or "being beside oneself." None of these kinds of disintegration or "falling apart" help in becoming happy.

Research on emotions reveals that humans can regulate emotions proactively by avoiding situations, stimuli, cues, or thoughts that bring undesired emotional responses. In an older language this process was called "avoiding the occasions of sin." Today's therapist may advise staying away from toxic relatives or destructive relationships. Prudent avoidance early avoids costly efforts later. Suppression is the hardest and least effective strategy. Studies of the ironic and contrary human mind have shown that a command produces an opposite reaction. "Don't think of white polar bears" is a negative command doomed to failure. After-the-fact reappraisals are also difficult.

In interventions aimed at becoming happy, the new research on self-regulation and emotion regulation can be articulated. But producing lasting changes can require a great deal of prolonged effort. Humans are so complex, it can take time and effort to entrain the multitude of conscious and nonconscious resources within us. "We are legion" is a human cry, but growing whole is a human possibility.

Achieving lasting happiness can require an individual's directed efforts over time and engagement with others. This developmental process has been called maturation, socialization, education, persuasion, conversion, or transformation. All consist of an effortful integration of a valued repertoire into a self-directed whole person. The guiding ideals of virtue or goodness or valued efforts that generate happiness will overlap in spiritual and psychological programs, but they all require individual choice and effort. Every religious, philosophical, and psychological therapeutic intervention understands that to become happy you have to let go or turn aside from short-term choices that don't work and which can bring misery to self and others. Self-direction and emotional self-regulation have to be achieved in order to realize lasting happiness.

When tempted to doubt the human capacity for emotional self-regulation and intentional change for the better, another related body of scientific evidence is significant. Neuroplasticity is the name given to recent explorations of the way that the human brain can be changed and rewired through individual effort and practice. Neuroplasticians are neuroscientists who have helped individuals retrain, rewire, or remap their brain structures through disciplined practice. Mostly these individuals have suffered brain injuries or other birth deficiencies formerly considered irreversible. In earlier, more static views of the brain, its neurons were considered to be so unchangeable that brain injuries or diseases were considered irremediable. Now the surprising potential for new neuron growth, called neurogenesis, has been discovered and stimulated exciting research. Unexpected potential for rewiring or creating new pathways within the brain have been found, and new connections result in recovered or new functions.

The findings that an adult can rewire the brain or have a brain that changes itself through conscious action appear revolutionary. It is an extraordinary example of the power of voluntary, sustained, self-directed action to change for the better. Positive physical changes of the body's muscle and physical functions through controlled exercise and diet have long been known, but voluntary self change or repair of one's own brain has not often been envisioned. Of course, without neuroimaging there could be no visual evidence of the powerful effects of conscious practice on the brain. Through autopsies, rats have been shown to have had their brain connections increased by placement in enriched environments, but they did not volunteer or exert conscious effort for the effects. It is now also accepted that experiences like learning languages can change human brains, but the amount and degree of change and rewiring taking place in the field of neuroplasticity is still hard to accept. The prolonged and strenuous efforts required to effect these therapeutic changes are also daunting.

Other new evidence of conscious self-changes in the brain has come from neurological research on the brains of individuals practicing advanced meditation, such as Buddhist monks and Christian nuns. Here, too, the brains of those who choose to practice prolonged meditation are observed to be different from the brains of controls who do not meditate. In deep states of meditation, subjective consciousness is reported to be altered and correlates with changing images of the brain. Other significant correlations with positive mental and physical health are found in those who meditate. However, these advanced meditators who showed changes in their brain and bodies had also practiced and persevered through long and arduous efforts of active focused meditation techniques and abstemious lifestyles. The control of attention in meditation requires persistent disciplined efforts, as anyone who tries it soon finds out. In a similar way, virtuous habits are not achieved in a day—a thought to remember when examining interventions for becoming happy.

Neuroplasticity and other brain research are in a fledgling state, as are the other strands of encouraging scientific research touched on above. I am reading this array of scientific evidence as woven into a web or entwined rope that supports human efforts to become happy. The new science of happiness is in my mind helping to empirically validate older spiritual truths. However, I never want to be self-deceived. So in the spirit of science and as a believer in God as truth as well as love, I remain open to disconfirming evidence. Having endorsed the emerging science of happiness as giving valuable support to spiritual and philosophical quests for happiness, I think it can be useful to examine some examples already on the scene. Two practical examples of programmed interventions aimed at becoming happy are ready at hand: the AA movement and a positive psychology how-to-become-happy self-guide.

The familiar AA movement promises to help individuals find a new happiness and a new joy in living. It emphasizes spirituality and a reliance on traditional religious wisdom. Positive psychologist Sonja Lyubomirsky presents a guided self-help program for becoming happy that draws upon the new psychological science of happiness. God is invoked in AA, and science in Lyubomirsky's guide. But in truth, both programs include a mix of interdisciplinary approaches, broad values, and psychological knowledge. Both also advocate moral values, virtue formation, spiritual practices, reasoned thinking found in science, and the use of effective psychological strategies. Conveniently, the AA program has its famous twelve steps and Lyubomirsky provides twelve happiness exercises. In both programs, becoming happy requires an individual's voluntary self-commitment and disciplined effort. Lasting changes come with resolve and perseverance, but success is promised.

Chapter 5

AA'S PATH TO HAPPINESS

Alcoholics Anonymous is a movement in which thousands of recovering alcoholics claim that they find "a new happiness." For many, the AA promise that they can become "happy, joyous, and free" comes true. This fulfillment is attributed by its members to the "spiritual awakening" received from practicing the AA twelve-step program. As AA's *Twelve Steps and Twelve Traditions* proclaims, "The joy of living is the theme of the Twelfth Step, and action is the key word." In *Alcoholics Anonymous*, known as the Big Book, which serves as the basic text of AA, the beginning chapters explain how the program works to bring sobriety. These descriptions of AA's principles and practices lead to forty-three personal stories of those who found "the road of happy destiny." While the twelfth step is the final one of the program, it is also seen as a beginning. For the rest of their sobriety, AA members seek to serve others and practice AA's spiritual principles "in all of their affairs." The primary goal is to stay sober and bring the message of hope to other alcoholics.

A commitment to helping others is one of the three basic principles of the program, of equal importance to recovery and unity. On the AA medallions given to those who achieve sobriety for ninety days, one year, two years, and onward, there is a triangle with the words "Recovery," "Unity," and "Service" embossed on the three sides. Recovery comes from practicing the steps or "working the program"; this is the "spiritual awakening" that brings sobriety and happiness. But what the alcoholic has received must be given back. To stay sober the recovering alcoholic engages in service and strives one day at a time for "progress, not perfection." As the alcoholic obsession and compulsion to drink lose their power, freedom from bondage results. Gradually, or sometimes suddenly, the craving for alcohol is lifted and self-destructive drinking ends. But the end of misery and "insanity" does not by itself fulfill AA's promise of becoming "happy, joyous, and free." Alcoholics who only achieve abstinence from alcohol without working the spiritual program are described as "dry drunks." The unique promise of happiness is fulfilled only as alcoholics begin to inwardly change their thoughts, emotions, and behavior.

Happiness and even sobriety are endangered unless personal changes take place; individuals must replace those ingrained patterns of response that can be easily triggered. In AA-speak, alcoholics can easily "pick up," "relapse," or "go out of the rooms." Only inner spiritual growth in honesty, service, prayer, and virtue can bring sobriety, one day at a time. The drama of every member's road to recovery begins with the way they came to work the AA program. In group meeting after group meeting, participants share the story of their painful descent into the misery of alcohol addiction until finally they reach a turning point. The downward path has as many starting points as there are unique people and existing life circumstances. Alcoholism is certainly no respecter of persons; people of every age, class, ethnicity, educational level, and family background can become ensnared, proving the adage that "alcoholism is an equal-opportunity disease." But familiar landmarks are passed on the road to addictive abuse of alcohol. Repeatedly, resolutions to stop getting drunk are broken, and troubles build up in every department of life. The endpoint is uncontrolled, self-destructive drinking. People describe how they "hit bottom," or arrived at the moment when they could no longer endure the sufferings that their drinking inflicted. They finally acknowledge personal powerlessness and become ready to give in and seek help. This readiness begins the journey of recovery. The turn to AA and the ascent to sobriety also display common characteristics.

The unity in diversity of the AA movement is based on the severity of the common problem and the uniformity of the twelve-step practices prescribed in the program. AA meetings with similar formats can be found in every state and region, as well as in many foreign countries. Since its founding in the 1930s, AA membership has increased to over a million people, and its programs are so widespread that groups can be found everywhere. Media and virtual forms of help are also available in telephone hotlines and chat rooms. The spiritual program is pursued in local AA home groups through regular routines (or rituals). These include reading aloud from authorized texts (as scripture), and voluntarily going around the room to share individual experiences in recovery (as witness and testimony). AA groups are free and open to all and self-supporting; a basket is passed (as a free-will offering). Service tasks are signed up for, such as leading meetings, making coffee, and running the self-governing business meetings. Members volunteer to sponsor new members or to go on outreach programs to hospitals and other groups (as on mission). At the end of each hourly meeting there is a brief closing prayer in a circle with linked hands; either the familiar serenity prayer or the Lord's Prayer is said in unison (as a benediction).

AA meetings provide immediate support through an equal acceptance of each individual who comes. To that end, no cross-talk, criticism, or judgments are countenanced; unconditional acceptance and affirmation are the rule. No one is ever pressured to speak if they choose to pass and simply listen. The rule of anonymity through the use of first names and initials only is pronounced. "Who you see here and what you hear here stays here." Honesty and openness are the professed ideals for the steps and for all contributions within the meeting. Often in meetings there will be spontaneous responses of empathy and encouragement, such as "Keep on coming," or other familiar AA slogans (or mantras). These slogans, along with the twelve steps and twelve traditions, are displayed on posters around the rooms; they can include, among others, "Think," "Live and let live," "Do the next right thing," "You are only as sick as your secrets," and above all, "One day at a time."

When a positive, trusting, and open atmosphere exists, the intimate support and approval of a home group is felt to be like that of a nurturing family or intimate circle of caring friends. Individuals share their fears, difficulties, struggles, and failures, as well as their "experience, strength, and hope." The group greets everyone by name and may applaud reports of abstinence achieved in the face of temptation, or clap for an individual's return to "the rooms" from a relapse. Meetings can include moving moments with tears and sympathetic groans, and even more invariably a great deal of laughter and joking.

Since AA meetings are so often depicted in the media (and satirized for their hokey language), the principles and practices of AA have entered into popular American culture. In addition to movies, TV, and plays, celebrities and talented writers regularly publish a plethora of recovery accounts. The story of an AA pilgrim's progress from the depths of suffering to the new happiness of sobriety includes an old but dramatic plot line. "I once was lost but now am found. Was blind but now I see." A lack of subtlety and nuance in AA's popular language or jargon (those corny rhymes) does not impede its power to affect enormous numbers of human lives.

So how exactly does the AA twelve-step program work to change lives and move persons from addiction to abstinence, from misery to happiness? That is the challenging and mysterious question not fully understood. Many explorations and explanations seeking answers describe the phenomenon in sociopsychological research projects as well as humanistic inquiries. These explorations might be divided roughly into those focusing on AA's spiritual dimension and those focused on its psychosocial dynamics. Happiness researchers do well to hone in on both characteristics as critically important.

Looking closely at the twelve-step spiritual program as well as the underlying psychological elements can produce insights for understanding the pursuit of happiness. In my judgment, AA's twelve-step program offers a remarkable synthesis of sound spiritual wisdom and effective therapeutic practices presented in a streamlined, condensed, and popularly accessible format. The program succeeds in presenting spiritual teachings with an underlying Christian character, interwoven with effective psychological therapeutics. Of course it doesn't work for everyone, but for thousands upon thousands who achieve sobriety in AA, the remarkable movement produces human flourishing and happiness. The AA program's characteristics can be examined to produce useful and general insights. After all, a person doesn't have to be a recovering alcoholic to become happy, joyous, and free. As a Christian psychologist and AA admirer, I try here to explore the program briefly—first through a religious lens and then from a psychological perspective.

AA's Twelve-Step Spirituality Program in a Christian Perspective

AA's program explicitly and clearly states that it aims at a "spiritual awakening" that will bring about a personal transformation. The capacity or power to experience this spiritual conversion is seen as a free gift from a Higher Power, or caring God, who will respond to a seeker's call for help. The Higher Power gives enabling power to a person who opens him- or herself to receive the gift of grace. As many observers have noted, the twelve-step program is founded upon and closely modeled on Christianity. This similarity comes as no surprise to anyone who knows about AA's history and the background of its remarkable cofounders. Both Bill W. and Dr. Bob were intelligent, attractive scions of upstanding New England families of Protestant origin. As young men, both had left behind their families' religious practices and gradually became hopelessly mired in the misery of midlife alcoholism. Uncontrollable drinking binges had brought both of them personal misery and career setbacks, sufferings shared with their families. While both Bill W. and Dr. Bob sought and received repeated treatment in medical rehabilitation programs, they continued to relapse. Eventually each sought spiritual help in an alliance with an emerging Christian movement, the Oxford group, founded with the goal of reviving the power and discipline of the early Christian church.

In a very short time the nascent AA movement separated from its explicitly Christian roots and began to focus exclusively on helping alcoholics recover. Yet overlapping memberships and support for AA continued for a good while. Other assistance and encouragement came from Christian clergymen and sympathetic physicians. In fact Bill W. was in a rehabilitation clinic for the fourth time when he experienced his overwhelming and transforming spiritual awakening. In desperation he had called upon God—if there was one—to help him. Instantly he was immersed in a shining sense of the presence of divine love and healing power. This decisive road-to-Damascus experience produced a dramatic recovery and decisively generated the spiritual path of the subsequent founding of the AA movement.

Deeply Christian faith elements became incorporated into the twelve-step spiritual program that Bill W. and Dr. Bob jointly crafted. Their aim was to be as inclusive as possible by stating that "AA is not aligned with nor endorses any sect, denomination, or political movement," and "has no criteria for membership but the desire to stop drinking." Yet the steps of AA closely follow the path and practices of Christian conversion and redemption. At the beginning of the first step, the alcoholic has to admit to being powerless over alcohol and acknowledge that his or her life has become unmanageable. The next step states that alcoholics "came to believe that a Power greater than ourselves could restore us to sanity." With this linguistic use of "we" and "us," the individual immediately becomes incorporated into a supportive fellowship that also depends upon access to the Higher Power's healing gifts. Step number three crucially moves to a "decision to turn our will and lives over to the care of God *as we understood Him.*" (Feminists cannot help but note that in AA's program, God is always referred to as He or Him as well as one's Higher Power.) This commitment to conform one's personal will to God's will brings with it the commitment to use one's human will, or what one *can* control, uprightly for good rather than for abuse. The commitment of giving away one's individual will paradoxically opens the person to receive the gift of God's power to move toward a changed life of sobriety. When in temptation, trouble, or indecision, the person can stop and pray the famous serenity prayer, "God grant me the serenity to accept the things I cannot change, the courage to change the things I can, and the wisdom to know the difference." Changing those things one can is a crucial acceptance of responsibility that requires effort as well as courage. The spiritual path to recovery and a new happiness begins step by step, one day at a time. AA claims it is a program of "progress, not perfection."

Similarly, a Christian believer who accepts Jesus Christ as savior, and who is baptized into the faith of the church, renounces the power of sin over self and receives God's power for salvation. A Christian begins the pilgrimage by being born again and participating in God's life. The faithful begin their transformation within the sacramental community of worship, committed to loving service of God and neighbor. The surrender of self to God's love allows the faithful to receive the power of the Holy Spirit; they become members of God's eternal family. The Christian must begin to "work out his salvation in fear and trembling" by following God's will for righteousness. These faith commitments result in actions large and small in a spiritual "sacrament of the present moment." The modeling of AA's spiritual program of recovery on Christian teaching is apparent. Most pointedly, the focus of both is on the present moment and on one day at a time.

Gradually, if and when AA's program is faithfully followed, it can bring a personal transformation from what is described as "self-centered narcissism" and "defiant individualism" to upright, sober, and joyful living in service for others. Members who work the program of steps learn to grow up or "meet life on life's terms." God as one's Higher Power is seen as able to remove all of a person's "character defects" if individuals "sincerely seek to have Him do so." As in a Christian examination of conscience, confession, and reparation, AA members engage in rigorous personal inventories and seek to make amends to all whom they have harmed. Working with a sponsor, past moral failures are listed and admitted to God and to another human being face to face. In later steps of the program, daily prayer and meditation are embraced. Daily moral guidance is sought to live soberly and serve others. "Sobriety" in AA language is used as a synonym for a fulfilled spiritual life in moral accord with God's will. Regular self-scrutiny and meditation encourage the individual to see things from another's point of view. When humility is practiced, one's own part in one's problems can be discerned and admitted; social difficulties with others subsequently begin to decline, and new vistas of living open up. One AA mantra claims that "more will be revealed" as one progresses in recovery. The ideal is the continuing growth in virtue and spiritual understanding.

Practicing AA's spiritual program entails not only individual meditation but also humbly seeking help from others more advanced than oneself. Choosing a sponsor is recommended since sponsors voluntarily guide and support the individual in carrying out the steps. This action reproduces the practice of having a novice master or spiritual director in the religious life. In any crises or difficulty, one's sponsor and an array of volunteer group members are available. Calling one's sponsor is a regular practice for many. The ups and downs of recovery can be made easier with support, both for newcomers and old-timers. Spiritual growth and understanding also come from faithfully attending AA meetings where one can contribute and listen to the insights of others. "Meeting makers make it" is the slogan. Making it in AA consists in living each day in honest, meaningful service and joyful recovery. Ethically, the AA spiritual program follows the basic Christian moral commandment: to love God and one's neighbor as oneself. Members accept the Golden Rule to do unto others as you would have them do to you. As practices of daily prayer and meditation increase, so do virtue, humility, and the desire to love and serve others. Here, in the emphasis upon prayer and service, the convergence with Christian belief and morality is most evident.

In the twelve steps, overt references to Christianity occur. For example, in the eleventh step—where contact with God is sought—the traditional prayer of Saint Francis is held up as a model to follow. In his famous prayer Francis asks to bring peace where there is strife, love where there is hate, hope where there is despair, and to always seek to "love rather than be loved." Francis affirms the gospel message that by forgiving one is forgiven.

One intriguing question that arises in the AA movement is why and how so many non-Christians, atheists, and agnostics remain loyal members of the fellowship despite its strong underlying Christian character.

Perhaps this is attributable to the plain, ordinary language used in the twelve-step program, which is also open enough and inclusive enough to accommodate religious nonbelievers. Moreover, in the AA steps, individuals are encouraged to employ their own understanding of their "Higher Power," which at a minimum can be seen as accepting that the power of the AA group is higher and stronger than that of the individual. "There may or may not be a God, but at least I know that I am not Him, Her, or It." AA literature also manages an empirical and experimental approach; skeptics are invited (like the first Christian disciples) to come and see. Test the program, and if it works for you, keep coming. If not, try it your way; you are always welcome to come back.

Nonbelievers can also stay because although Christian spirituality interpenetrates the steps, the program also includes tried-and-true moral truths found in many different wisdom traditions. For instance, the Greco-Roman classical virtues of prudence, justice, temperance, and courage were quickly incorporated into early church teachings. In actuality, as extended study of other civilizations and cultures have shown, universal moral truths and ethical maxims exist as guides to behavior. Nonbelievers can accept AA's universal moral truths, such as "Know thyself," "Be truthful," "Seek the counsel of the wise and good," "Follow your conscience," and, with the Buddhists, "Be attentive and mindful in the present moment."

AA inherits much of the practical common sense of a democratic culture inspired by American Protestantism. AA's governing traditions—from openness, voluntarism, and democratic leadership, with rotating terms for jobs and adherence to a flexible group conscience—reflect the legacy of its founders' Congregationalist traditions. These faiths had inspired the grassroots democracy of the New England town meeting. Calvinism also had a hardy concept of human sin and fallibility, which is also at work in much of the prudential and sagacious rules of AA's twelve traditions. While the tradition of anonymity protects individual privacy and encourages openness and trust, it also ensures that individuals do not use the movement for personal aggrandizement or economic gain. Scriptural injunctions to not let the left hand know what the right hand does serve the same purpose of guarding against hypocritical pride and status seeking. Anonymity helps to get the self out of the way; it helps support the AA tradition of letting "principles not personalities" be the rule.

The completely voluntary and democratic practices of the AA movement, so akin to early church practices, refute those critics who accuse AA of being a self-serving cult that is perniciously closed in upon itself and maintained by hypnotic conditioning. The telltale characteristics of religious cults are their authoritarian insistence on obedience to narrowly doctrinaire beliefs and a hostility to anyone outside the group. But it seems off the mark to accuse AA of removing its members from the larger society. From its very beginnings to the present, AA has encouraged the use of medical consultations and professional therapeutic experts familiar with alcoholism. Group members often enter psychotherapy or adopt spiritual advisors from their home churches. Cooperation with religious denominations prevails as it did at AA's inception. In fact, newfound sobriety often inspires members to return to their religious roots and early faith communities. As a final proof, simply count the enormous number of AA meetings taking place in church basements.

Moreover, in contrast to the problematic practices of many cults, AA offers no financial profit for any leader or anyone else involved. Those who carry out the organizational work to keep a local group going are volunteers who serve on a rotating basis. All outreach, sponsorships, and other service work is done by volunteers dedicated to service. These open procedures curtail the chances for abuses of power. As for the supposedly cultlike "brainwashing" that opponents see operating in AA, this can be a negatively biased perception of the tools necessary to achieve recovery's freedom from addiction. Older self-destructive habits and attitudes have to be changed to achieve sobriety. To change requires new thoughts, new emotional responses, and new behaviors in a disciplined effort. These are learned and sustained by new and repeated routines and practices inspired in group meetings.

Members see the ritual of giving one's first name and identification as an alcoholic, followed by a greeting from the group, as a reminder of the addictive hold of alcohol over individuals and the power of group healing. Denial is overcome by humility, defined as the ability to remain teachable. Alcoholics have done themselves great harm by making exceptions in their own "terminally unique" cases. Relearning bad habits and coping with ingrained automatic responses is not easy; initially it requires vigilant self-awareness. This raised consciousness is necessary to sense old dangers and acquire new countercues, prompts, and reactions. The relearning may be helped along by using easy-to-remember, simplistic tags and slogans. For instance, HALT stands for the fact that the alcoholic's risk of relapse is greater when he or she is Hungry, Angry, Lonely, or Tired.

Other simple rituals, prompts, and phrases can work for members no matter their level of education. Perhaps the most educated, accomplished, wealthy, professional medical and religious leaders have the most difficulties in overcoming their defensiveness and admitting their need for help. (Just as it is as hard for a rich person to be saved as for a camel to go through the eye of a needle?) Wholehearted assent is necessary but not easy, yet external coercion won't work. Only inner desire can motivate sustained effort. AA emphasizes repeatedly that it is a movement of attraction, not promotion. As with Christianity, conversion requires voluntary practices.

Another perennial pitfall to be avoided in AA lies in the human temptation for the converted to try to control others for their own good. A built-in principle of the AA program counters this tendency. The asserted belief is that all individuals have their own Higher Power, so their spiritual path to recovery is their own responsibility. A measure of detachment follows because no one can make another sober or keep a person from relapse. On the AA medallion, the maxim written around the motto "Recovery, Unity, and Service," is "To Thine Own Self Be True," an ultraindividualistic mandate that balances the communal "we" consciousness of the movement.

Another instance of AA's self-affirming focus is the program's declaration that recovering alcoholics are helping themselves as they help others. The claim is that AA members stay sober through service to other alcoholics—whether their efforts succeed or not. The understanding that an individual receives benefits from helping others has been called "the helper principle" and is seen as one foundation of innate human altruism. This emphasis has fortunate side effects: no one needs to worry whether any service effort will achieve success, nor should they feel competitive over the number of people helped compared to others. Best of all, the recipients of help do not need to be shamed, obligated, or burdened with debt. After all, they are actually doing the AA member a favor. Altruistic "twelve-stepping" benefits the helper. Indeed, the concept that giving is getting is found in many spiritual traditions, as in the above reference to the prayer of Saint Francis. In the Gospels, Christ teaches that "it is more blessed (or joyful) to give than to receive." Jesus tells his disciples, "The Son of Man has come to serve, not to be served."

Those AA members who continue to "work the program" are rewarded in finding meaning and happiness through serving others. They gain a new freedom and a sense of joyful purpose. Individuals who positively engage with valued others find their lives enlarged and enhanced. Becoming a member of a group that shares good work and good times is satisfying and attracts others. Similarly, the mutual love, equality, and support of the early Christian house churches magnetically attracted converts—especially women and slaves. To this day, small Christian base communities re-create the early house church experiences. So, too, in AA, home-group meetings can have a churchlike fellowship of thankfulness and praise for the gifts the Higher Power grants. Enthusiasm, high spirits, and a soaring sense of gratitude often pervade meetings. Christian spiritual writers describe how the gathered faithful, recalling all of life's good gifts, can experience gratitude welling up and escalating into a "high" of joy. Pentecostal groups proceed to speak in tongues and be slain in the Spirit. But even the more reserved faithful may discern the Holy Spirit's presence when their "hearts burn within them."

AA groups can generate a "high" of gratitude that is expressed in joyful laughter and affection. Joy, like other emotions, is contagious and serves to increase the healing power of AA groups. In religious faith healing, the gathered members pray, praise, give thanks, and lay hands upon the ill to bring about a cure. In AA the laying on of hands takes the form of occasional hugs but more often of verbal forms of support and offers of personal telephone numbers to call when in need. This group support can operate between meetings as well.

In Christian spirituality the aid of those in the church existing beyond death is envisioned as remaining available; these invisible helping ones are referred to as the "cloud of witnesses." The holy friends and family of God continue to care and exert influence on behalf of the progress of the pilgrim church on earth. Similarly, an imagined AA group residing in the mind's eye can exert influence on a member who is tempted to relapse. "How sad my group will be if I pick up now, and how proud they will be if I resist this temptation."

An AA home group's positive influence can be long-lasting. Members come and go, but the stable core of a local group grows old together. "Old-timers" can be role models for others when they "die sober," or as expressed in religious terms, die a "good death," faithful to the end. While aging and death assail everyone and narrow one's life, those on a spiritual pilgrimage can take heart; they are open to an infinite horizon. Who is ever done with growing in prayer, increasing in love, or gaining in wisdom? Engaging activities with others or the Other are known as "together goods," or those goods that only emerge in interrelationships. Spiritually growing avoids stagnation and boredom; altruistic efforts move beyond the self and bring stimulation, openness, and novelty. A spiritual path, however rocky, is enlivening and "spirited." AA's program is based on "together goods" that lead to happiness.

In a more formal analysis, AA's spiritual program can be theologically seen as the work of God's Holy Spirit, which sustains and renews creation. The Christian triune God of love is one who makes all things new. God is "divine liveliness," or the infinite source of the deepest energy of the world. The Holy Spirit is known to work always and everywhere to draw creatures Godward and into God's communal life filled with truth and joy. Those who see AA as a work of the Holy Spirit consider it fitting that traditionally the Holy Spirit is known as the anonymous person of the Trinity. In AA or elsewhere, the spirit born of love is constantly enlivening the hearts and minds of individuals and groups that are open to God's goodness. Where "two or three are gathered together in my name," says Jesus, the Spirit's beneficent power can be manifested. The stipulation of "in my name" can be viewed as inclusive, applying to all those groups, like AA, dedicated to God's work of transformation and healing. The traditional gifts and fruits of God's Holy Spirit have been seen as love, joy, peace, self-control, patience, courage, and counsel, among other good traits that lead to human flourishing.

The traditional works of mercy empowered by the Spirit have been denoted as admonishing, comforting, counseling, instructing, forgiving, and meeting concrete bodily human needs. AA's altruistic twelve-stepping or service to others can be seen as works of mercy involving all of the Spirit's gifts. Anonymous or not, the transforming fruits of the Holy Spirit can be identified in AA. In addition, Christian members of AA regularly see "miracles" take place. Group members observe newcomers of every stripe and persuasion drag into meetings in various states of mental, emotional, and physical disarray. Then slowly over time, those who persevere or "keep on coming" to work the program show visible and positive change in face, body posture, language, mood, and behavior. Another life is turned around. As one young woman recalled in a meeting, "My friend met me and said he was glad to see that death had lost its power over me." In AA an alcoholic's road to death can be reversed, and the path to happiness embraced. As others have said, "I was miserably enslaved but now am free." But then, should not the faithful expect to see joy increase when persons seek closeness to the God or Higher Power who promises a kingdom in which "every tear will be wiped away"?

As argued in the chapter on religious approaches to happiness, Christians affirm that we live within a basically good but still unfinished, skewed creation groaning into its new birth; present sufferings from addiction, disease, sin, and oppression are destructive powers that can be overcome. AA's spiritual program provides another vivid witness that God's gift of happiness can be enjoyed here and now—in unlikely circumstances, with unlikely people. Looking around in AA meetings one can echo what was once noted of the church: "Here comes everybody."

Maybe so, but is the AA spiritual path too wide and the gate set too low to be in accord with Christianity? What do those advocates of AA answer to critics who object to AA's referring to God as our "Higher Power" or "God as we understood Him"? Don't these phrases have the ring of a vague, new-age pseudoreligion? In AA's defense I can point out that in orthodox Christianity no human can ever possess more than the most partial understanding of God, the ineffable divine mystery. The transcendent divine Creator will always be beyond human thought or imagination. Christian faith affirms that God dwells in unapproachable light, and no words or definitions can ever comprehend the incomparable ground of all being. Confronting the divine fountain of plenitude, human creatures are always going to have to rely on a limited intuition, or approach God as we inadequately manage to understand the Holy One.

Yet there is another pole of the revealed Christian message; the scriptures proclaim that God is love and seeks an irreversible bonded relationship with all God's beloved creatures. Creation is God's self-bestowal of love. God is simultaneously and transcendently beyond all human imagination while also inwardly present everywhere. God lives within human beings, closer to us than we are to ourselves. In the incarnation God in Jesus becomes fully human and fully divine, thereby irreversibly bonded with humankind. God as love seeks communion with God's beloved creatures, giving and receiving love. The humility and noncoercive self-bestowal of God-love in the universe seeks the freedom and happiness of humankind. Infinite mercy for all, no matter their status, is proclaimed in the prophetic words: "a bruised reed I will not break nor a flickering wick extinguish."

Such unconditioned mercy and love do not bespeak a God who would reject an appeal for help because it is tentatively addressed to "my Higher Power." In Jesus' great parable of the Prodigal Son, the father does not wait to be addressed or receive an apology but runs to embrace him in joy. It is also instructive to remember that Jesus in the jostling crowds

felt his healing touch go out from him to cure the foreign Syrophoeni-
cian woman—even though she did not even have the temerity to address
him. Her inner movement of hope and faith was answered. Healing is
offered to all.

AA's promises fulfilled are seen by Christians to be examples of divine
gifts freely given to all the creation, but this affirmation doesn't mean
that the faithful stop trying to understand how these healing processes
operate. For those who believe that the God of love is the God of truth,
intellectual efforts to understand the world's realities give further glory
to God the Creator. Human beings made in the image of God as created cocreators have been accorded the "dignity of causing" and invited
to participate in transforming the world into God's good kingdom.
Believers desire to use their God-given talents of rationality, intuition,
intelligent imagination, insight, and creative problem solving to find
God in all things. The discoveries of science and technology give praise
to the Creator, just as worship, art, music, literature, theology, humane
studies, and charity do.

For those who affirm that the "proper study of man is man," nothing
seems more intriguing and vitally important than to understand the way
human minds, hearts, and behavior can change for the good. Christian
psychologists like myself affirm that God acts through the lawfulness
and the contingencies of the creation but that we by no means understand all the amazing operations of the universe. The great intellectual
challenge lies in analyzing dynamic human realities that exist at every
level and dimension of reality. The potent psychosocial operations in
AA that lead to sobriety and happiness are important to note and attempt to understand.

Psychosocial Dimensions in AA's Twelve-Step Program

An earlier chapter on the science of happiness gave a brief account of
the scientific grounding for claims that human beings can change for the
better and become happy, or at least, happier. The chapter specifically
devoted to positive psychology's self-help programs presents a discussion

of new psychological findings. Here I do not repeat these points but take a closer look at three of AA's more intriguing psychological dynamics: the powerful role of the group, the powerful effect of sharing personal stories, and the powerful role of empathy and positive emotions. These may be among the mysterious operative ingredients that most help bring about the positive personal change that produces happiness. If so, then other pursuits of happiness and transformation outside of AA may do well to imitate them.

The Power of the Group

Face-to-face groups have been the subject of enormous amounts of research in social science and psychology. Whole courses in group dynamics are offered in different psychological domains exploring in detail the interactions of group members and the operations of groups over time. Group therapy is studied and contrasted with individual approaches. Why so much attention? Clearly, so much research is given to this topic because groups exert incredible influence upon every aspect of an individual's life—for both good and ill. In our evolutionary past the primates who emerged as Homo sapiens lived in small bands within a threatening and dangerous environment. Individual members of the groups depended upon the group for survival, as well as for all other pleasurable social human activities. Other animals and insects also have evolved herd instincts or hive instincts, but in humans this drive to belong to the group can become a conscious as well as an unconscious programmed motivation. Imitation and synchronous and emotionally contagious activity are instinctually part of group survival operations. To be rejected, isolated, or abandoned by the group spelled death and dehumanization.

But why should we be surprised? Individual members of the species to this day depend upon groups for infant survival, child health, successful socialization, and effective adult functioning. Early family nurturing and participation in a succession of groups throughout an extended life cycle determine an individual's destiny. In an increasingly complex environment, individuals are shaped by numerous groups: nuclear families, kith and kin, childhood peers, schoolmates, colleagues, civic organizations, churches, and other overlapping mediating institutions that exist between the individual and the nation-state. Human well-being depends upon and is definitively shaped through groups from the nursery to the nursing home.

Unfortunately the power of groups can operate in detrimental and destructive ways. Abusive families, bullying schoolmates, youthful gangs, adult mobs, or military units can behave more aggressively together than they would as individuals. Scapegoats and victims of group violence remain a fact of modern life—and one reason that social scientists study groups. More subtle forms of exclusion and hostility also mark the destructive operations of some groups. On the other hand, supportive, caring groups can exert primary nurturing and other abundantly positive effects on individuals. Development and change for the good is brought about in nurturing families. Later, therapeutic effects take place in religious cell groups, educational training groups, rehabilitation teams, psychological therapy, and of course, self-help groups and AA. The important challenge is to find out how positive groups bring about their good effects. In therapy groups it isn't just a matter of a more efficient use of resources and the savings of money and time compared to a one-to-one interaction. Face-to-face groups provide advantages, especially those groups sharing a common goal and giving members an equal voice.

Group participants can be more ready to listen to one another's advice than to that of a more removed authoritarian leader. Members can provide each other with information, spontaneous feedback, and emotional support that is credible when it comes from a number of peers. Best of all, those who make progress encourage others by their success. "If they can do it, I can do it." Reciprocally, any help individuals can give to one another buoys their own morale and sense of self-worth. Groups give an opportunity for reciprocal altruism with all of its positive effects. Attentive listening as a benign, supportive audience is by itself a gift of participants to one another.

When attentive groups build up trust in one another, as the rule of confidentiality is followed, members feel free to disclose their problems and failures as well as their successes. Mutually sharing a personal private world with its moral struggles provides mutual enlightenment. These privileged disclosures cannot help but be extremely fascinating to our curious fellow humans. What are these other people thinking and feeling? To enter the hidden inner worlds of inner consciousness requires inviting others to know what is going on behind the eyes. Nonverbal clues can convey much, but only so much. What is the real story or the backstory? In our media culture, a plethora of television interviews, blogs, reality shows, published memoirs, magazine articles, and newspaper stories attempts answers. But in bonded groups the honest and humble verbal self-disclosure goes deeper and cuts to the bone. Communication at a deep and serious level can make more conventional exchanges pale by comparison. Conversations about moral and personal concerns are a rare commodity and privilege. A group that practices openness, honesty, humility, equality, and attentive listening provides stimulating and bracing experiences.

A lot of vicarious learning can take place in a group setting through observation and imitation. Listening to others as they reflect and interact allows observing individuals to learn. Comments and reflections from others stimulate one's own thinking and self-examination. Idealistic aspirations are admired and appropriated. Timely warnings about pitfalls of the road to the goal of transformation can be heeded, as well as news of victories. Learning new thought processes and patterns of thinking are a great part of an AA group's therapeutic effectiveness. While it is doubtful that words and thoughts without emotional support can be as effective as both together, the power of confronting and revising older thoughts and habitual thought patterns is crucial for therapeutic change. The AA term "stinking thinking" is used for the negative, destructive thought patterns that afflict individuals and lead to relapse and addiction. Airing these patterns and hearing them corrected or challenged—or laughed at with familiar recognition—is part of the group learning. The approved AA texts help because they alert readers to perilous cognitive responses leading to self-deception, as well as recommending effective strategies. Repetition reiterates these lessons, and group testimonies confirm them.

Part of restoring hope and self-worth comes from adopting new attitudes about what is possible and how one should judge behaviors—failings and successes. How dysfunctional emotions can be regulated becomes explicitly discussed. Like the approach of the cognitive behavior therapy movement, AA groups can discuss how different attributions and explanations of behavior can cause different emotional and behavioral reactions. A new thought and a new self-awareness give a new potential for change. Groups help members tap into insights on the effects of changing your perspective or interpretation. When I make a mistake it can be viewed as a temporary setback that effort can rectify, or seen as the inevitable proof of my inept and hopeless condition. So why not take a drink? Accounts of monumental feats of self-deceptive thinking regularly provoke peals of laughter in AA meetings, although the results are never funny.

In therapy groups, the range and variety of members present can broaden the learning process and strengthen the insights and testimony available. AA as a movement attracts a wide swath of Americans, to good effect. So many citizens live in fairly narrow social niches filled with people of a similar age, class, income, education, religion, and political ideology. These constrained vistas can be expanded with profit. Middle-class, educated types learn quickly that individuals from every social sphere and background can offer impressive words of wisdom and sensitivity. Social and emotional intelligence prove to be more helpful than high IQ, high income, or high status. In egalitarian AA groups the productive rule is that everyone is welcome; everyone is to be accepted and listened to with courtesy and lack of criticism.

Surely the magnetic attraction and healing power of the AA movement produces the transformative experiences found in mutually supportive groups. It's no accident that social movements of every ideological stripe have gained influence and exerted social power through small group organization. From Plato's academy to early Christian house churches, from communist cells to feminist consciousness-raising groups, from political reform clubs to terrorist cells, dynamic energies and purposeful creative strategies are generated within groups. Groups change individuals, and individuals change groups. Groups support individuals, and both act to change the world. This group energy has been named "synergy" because a group exists as more than the sum of its parts, more than an aggregate of individuals. A group emerges as an existing entity when interpersonal interactions take place and bonds emerge between participants. Groups are marked by mutual influence, such as contagious emotions, creative thinking, concentrated energies, and increased commitment to act collectively (both positively and negatively). When group power is used for the good, healing energies are released. The AA program expresses this truth in its maxim: "Together we can do what we can never do alone."

The human capacity for imaginatively constructing images and memories means that a group's imagined existence can affect an individual when the group is physically absent. As mentioned above in the Christian concept of an invisibly encouraging "cloud of witnesses," the envisioning of the AA group remembered between meetings can shore up resistance to relapse. A group residing in one's head or in working memory can affect an individual's behavior in many ways, especially in times of stress, conflict, or temptation. William James wrote of the mind's ability to construct an ideal group of witnesses that would validate you and strengthen your resolution when hard-pressed in some present circumstance. This kind of imaginative construct can be at work when embattled West Point graduates invoke "the long gray line" who've gone before. And when it comes down to it, a little self-scrutiny unveils the various groups that live in our own heads. Other cultures also have such groups, perhaps consisting of "the ancestors," or the clan's "guardian spirits." In these cases the power of the group can be seen to be profoundly based upon the compelling emotional desire to live up to the group's standard. Each human being comes programmed with an innate sense of "we," which allows a group to powerfully change them. But in some cases like AA, another factor can be operating.

The Power of Telling One's Story

In many a therapeutic group, but especially in AA, members are invited to tell their story—over and over again. Regular participants of AA are asked to identify with and offer their responses to AA texts or to a meeting's featured speaker. Or they will be asked to volunteer to be the featured speaker. After having passed a probationary period of sobriety—say, 90 days—a person can be invited to go on outreach visits to rehabilitation centers or other groups to speak. Over and over, individuals relate the story of their growing addiction to alcohol and their path to their Higher Power and AA. To tell this story, a person must be willing to look homeward to their family beginnings and development through youth and adulthood to construct a narrative. Another review of the personal story is required when an individual is "working the steps" and must list the people one has harmed over one's life in order to make amends to them. When further in the program and seeking to have their character flaws removed, more life review is indicated. As self-scrutiny and careful efforts to grow proceed, the habitual practice of the self-examined life becomes the norm. Those nonattended habits, reflexes, socially pressured emotional responses, and chance events will come into explicit consciousness. Inchoate, unfocused, nonaware functioning becomes explicitly observed. Or as the Freudians would put it in their system, "Where there is id, let ego be."

Getting to know one's multidimensioned, partly nonconscious self is not a simple or quickly completed task. Defense and denial can be an impediment. Moreover, individuals are always changing as they move through time and social space. But constantly telling and retelling your story involves revising and deepening the insights, interpretations, and perspectives brought to bear on your past development. And as the wry comment has it, the past is not even past. The past as remembered in the present can be changed. One way this happens is in cultivating forgiveness for those who have wronged you. Laying to rest old resentments by new understandings of my part and that of others in my story can remove obsessions that consume energy. Repenting, making amends, and forgiving others and oneself bring peace of mind and an openness to a new chapter in one's life story.

Exercising directed consciousness to one's personal story within a group, with a sponsor, or while alone induces self-reflection, and over time a realization that one is changing. One amusing feature of AA meetings is regularly hearing how puzzled or even hostile a newcomer felt on first hearing all the group talk about "spirituality." "It really didn't make much sense to me at the time, but I wanted what you had, so I kept coming." Later, when understanding increases, individuals readily accept the fact that wherever they now are on their journey, it will continue. Buddhist maxims can be offered such as "more will be revealed" or "when the student is ready, the teacher will appear." But it should by rights be "teachers" in the plural. Mutually attentive listening to everyone's story results in a creative collective process. Individuals become more uniquely and distinctly conscious selves as they become more conscious of being members of a community. Increasing self-conscious awareness is known to stimulate efforts to live up to the self's moral and social standards. Communicating with others enables communicating with oneself with positive results.

Inevitably and inexorably, those who participate in the program construct an integrated life history, or a psychological, social, and spiritual resume, that is coherent. This individualistic construction of one's own narrative is achieved within a supportive accepting group that is telling their own stories. The result is a constantly interweaving tapestry of unique individual accounts within a group consciousness. A balance is struck between uniqueness and group unity. Back to those words on the AA medallion that read, "Unity, Recovery, and Service," surrounded by the motto, "To Thine Own Self Be True." To be true to self in AA's spiritual program clearly means to acquire virtue and a relationship with God. The group consciousness is identified with the group conscience, or commitment to goodness and sobriety. Truly sober persons are morally and spiritually awakened and upright, practicing virtuous principles in all of their affairs. As listeners hear and tell these stories, they can take hope for themselves and others suffering from alcoholism. They can also see reiterated the common elements of becoming happy and free. AA is the land of happy endings.

As one's life story is repeated in audiences where there is attentive listening, acceptance, and mutual sharing, a person's self-confidence grows. As others accept you, you grow to accept yourself. Hearing your own story from the audience's point of view, some distance is gained even while immediately engaged in the telling. Gradually, self-awareness can increase and at the same time become more congruent with those spontaneous, nonconscious parts of one's self. Awareness brings the capacity for self-control. Patterns become clearer as an integrated, comprehensible account is constructed. Those things you could not control can be assigned to chance, and responsibility can be assumed for what one has done with the cards one was dealt. One's personhood and one's place in time and history emerge and can be owned and accepted. In the scriptures, Saint Paul at one point cries out in a letter to his friends and followers, "I am who I am." I wonder whether this cry might be echoing Yahweh's words to Moses to tell his people that he has met "I AM WHO I AM," or in some translations, "I AM WHO WILL BE." Echo or not, it can at least be concluded that the Higher Power is in favor of becoming a person. On a less sublime and more ridiculous note, it can be remembered that Popeye the Sailor Man also constantly asserted, "I yam who I yam." Humility means you remain teachable but also that you accept your story, and can look to the open future.

In telling AA stories you can also, like Saint Paul and Popeye, use your past ups and downs to help others. Past failures can be turned to good account when disclosures give warning as well as encouragement to the wayfarer. Those who have shared the darkness can be heard. This is an example of what has been called the "wounded healer effect." Perhaps more fortunately, those who tell their story to benefit others will reap the reward that follows upon altruistic helping. The helper principle ensures that helping others raises the giver's morale. Altruism makes us happy, just as accomplishing or achieving goals gives us a positive reward. This feeling of self-efficacy produces innate satisfactions that begin in infancy and last the rest of life. It is particularly satisfying when unfortunate events, failures, and misdeeds can be turned to good purpose. Mutual happiness is enlarged with heartfelt gratitude.

The stories told in AA are narratives filled with gratitude. It is inevitable even though it is often repulsive to newcomers: "I thought if I heard one more person say, 'I am a grateful recovering alcoholic,' I'd puke." But gratitude has many uses, and can relate to tales of good things received as well as bad things removed. No more miserable hangovers, no more arrests for driving while intoxicated, and no more financial, work, or family disasters incurring guilt. Gratitude also preempts resentments, envy, anger, and irritable agitation. It works against the so-called hedonic treadmill. This idea asserts that no matter how many good things are enjoyed, soon enough they will be taken for granted as adaptation builds up and bored dissatisfaction increases. The theory is that more and more positive stimuli are needed to get the hedonic effect to work. But if gratitude surges with each telling of the rescue story, then it will be renewable and fill the present moment to the brim. No room for irritable agitation, serenity will abound. Gratitude, of course, is often explicitly religious as the faithful daily give God thanks and praise; this gratitude may be one reason that religious believers are so often found to be happy. But gratitude can have a secular equivalent as well. Thankfulness *for* rather than thankfulness *to* a divine Giver can be offered. In either case, gratitude and other positive emotions bring happiness. That leads us to the core and most highly effective path to becoming happy: the power of positive emotions.

The Power of Empathy and Positive Emotions

In earlier chapters I discussed the new emphasis upon the psychology of emotion and the discovery of the centrality of empathy. Here again it's important to note that positive emotions can most unfailingly be generated in good company and like all emotions are contagious. Fear, anger, and sorrow have long been known to be "catching," but now positive emotions like joy, interest, and love are, too. Positive merriment and delighted laughter ripple through groups accompanied by affection. Mothers and babies begin the innate human story of intimate empathic knowing and loving. Adult lovers and friends continue to seek and find the intersubjective consciousness and bonding that gives joy. Adult experiences of love follow the template of earlier joy, security, and satisfaction that infants provide when they are fed, cared for, and played with by a nurturing mother. The best news about the human species is that positive intersubjective experiences of love and interest generate a sense of self in infancy through a process of becoming that continues throughout life. Philosophers and theologians have noted the power of "I-Thou" or "face-to-face" relationships to validate and confirm the reciprocal equal value of human beings. Today, psychology and social neuropsychology with its new research on mirror neurons and on mother-infant studies confirm realities that older spiritual wisdom and religious understanding have proclaimed.

Here I want to focus specifically on the power of positive emotions and empathy to bring about positive change in individuals and groups. AA is a prime example of the transformations possible. The emotional caring and support given by others in a group or in one-to-one sponsor-sponsee relationships satisfies the universal desire for valued acceptance and authentic caring. Always and everywhere individuals desire to be valued for themselves and genuinely appreciated as having dignity among equals. The thirst to be known for who one really is and the desire to be loved by others are intense. When you have these desires fulfilled it is like finding water in the desert. AA exerts its influence on individuals mainly in my judgment through the group's proffering of empathy and positive emotions.

Empathy is vital to human flourishing as the innate human capacity that enables one individual to feel as another does and then to sympathize with that person. The innate positive emotions are recognized as the various good expressions of joy, interest, and love. In other words, empathy and positive emotions make human life worthwhile.

The importance of empathy and positive emotion was not always fully recognized in recent decades in either medicine, psychology, or psychotherapy. Therapeutic efforts tended to focus mostly on disordered negative emotions such as fear, anger, sorrow, guilt, shame, and so on. This asymmetry of interest can be understood since so much suffering is caused by the malfunction of negative emotions. Until recently, research on the positive and healing effects of positive emotions was all but non-existent. Priority was given to relieving harmful negative dysfunctions rather than attending to proactive or preventive strategies that employ and engender positive emotions. AA's spiritual, proactive program focusing on positive spiritual growth can be seen as a happy exception to the rule. Even so, its emphasis upon exactly how proactive, prosocial emotions and responses operated was little analyzed. But even in AA, a certain bias toward negative emotional factors can be discerned.

A reigning assumption in AA, and in other therapy programs, has been that only the negative build-up of pain and suffering motivates a person to seek help and turn to AA. The alcoholic, it is said, must first "hit bottom" and experience complete defeat and powerlessness in order to finally act. Well, yes, surely pain and negative emotions in general serve as a universal signal that some behavior is in need of a course correction, but this is only part of the story. It is also true that pain and suffering alone are not always enough to motivate and initiate efforts to change. Alcoholics, like other chronic sufferers, can become inured to their misery and helplessness. They can continue to drink destructively, no matter the cost. Unfortunately, prolonged suffering can wear people down and cast them into apathetic despair. Abused women, tortured prisoners, the starving, or mistreated children can sink into depressed apathy and learned helplessness. In learned helplessness, individuals have given up trying to escape since past efforts have been hopeless. Overcoming paralysis takes some intimation of a new possibility emerging into consciousness to motivate the movement to seek help. A positive response follows from some positive new feeling of hope. At the same time there must be some positive affirmation of the self that says, "Yes, even I am worth saving." In prevailing darkness a glimmer of light must enter to illuminate and change the scene. The positive pull of a future good motivates movement toward the promise of help; one surrenders. The spiritual and psychological surrender that initiates AA's twelve-step program is not a negative or passive resignation but rather an active willingness to give a benevolent Higher Power a chance to work.

Psychologically, the rescue from despairing powerlessness can be seen to spring from a person's positive move beyond the barricaded self—outward, upward, over, and around entrenched defenses. Christian believers see this turn to God's power as a manifestation of the magnetic power of God's love drawing the human spirit Godward. A psychosocial analysis notes the way a shift of attention toward the Higher Power and the group can give a self-besieged person space to breathe. The self's constricted field of play is broadened as the number of players increases in the game. The first steps in AA simultaneously produce a new relationship with God or a Higher Power, and with a supportive group of peers. Group interactions within a broader framework inevitably begin to operate and initiate change. Being accepted despite one's impotence and fallibility opens up a healing interpersonal process. Positive acceptance from others challenges obsessive self-laceration and depressed fatalism. Receiving unconditional acceptance from a Higher Power and the nonjudgmental empathy of fellow alcoholics allows defenses to be relaxed. Risking an openness to new attitudes and new behaviors becomes possible. A person can be buoyed up by positive emotional acceptance. As so many in AA have said, "When I come into these rooms I feel at home."

Only in recent decades have the healing and energizing effects of positive emotions begun to be understood generally. The healing power of AA, in my judgment, comes from its altruistic caring fellowship based upon the emotional bonding of positive emotions. Empathy, sympathy, joy, interest, and love effect the personal transformation. In the new psychological research under way, positive emotions are described as broadening and building. They broaden a person's attention and build engagement with the social and natural environment. The pleasure and enjoyment experienced make continuing response effortless. Positive pleasure felt in the beauty of nature seems to be as innate in humans as love and enjoyment of the company of others. Joy, love, and interest direct attention magnetically to what is enjoyed and valued. Positive feelings of pleasure and delight sustain the activities that are savored.

When individuals feel joy they become open and trusting. Being accepted and valued is being secure and safe. When positively relaxed and pleasured, it is easy to explore new ideas and new ways of thinking. With the advent of positive new responses, previous negative patterns can begin to be mitigated, replaced, and overridden, and thus they fade away. These effects of positive emotions are the reason persons are able to undo ingrained negative responses. Positive emotions of joy and love in therapy and in ordinary life experiences can begin to heal trauma and other emotional disasters. Resilience accompanies new interests and new experiences with good persons and good times. Enjoyable, satisfying new response patterns and connections are repeated and sustained. Over time, positive emotional responses can replace self-defeating responses and become habitual. Flexible humans learn, develop, become conditioned and reconditioned, and rewire their plastic brains. In maturing and learning processes a normal adult individual can partially direct conscious attention through executive functions or acts of will. Individuals can strive for goals, engage in practice, and gradually find that new behavior can become automatic and incorporated into one's personality. The AA slogan or directive, "Fake it 'til you make it," is a shorthand reference to the promise that persons can partially change themselves.

Another new and intriguing line of research on positive emotion that is pertinent to their transformative and healing effects is their power to restore depleted egos. Ego depletion theories posit that personal psychological selves can become fatigued and depleted of energy, just like physical powers. After long, hard periods of controlled attention, a person's efforts of concentration, will, or executive function begin to falter and weaken. Certain kinds of effortful work, study, or controlled activity may deplete psychological resources. Some of these efforts may involve moral self-control or self-management. They take a toll on energy also. As the executive ego's willed energy is exerted over an extended time it grows depleted. Then resistance to distraction lowers, and relief and release are sought. A person becomes vulnerable to temptation.

An awareness of these psychological processes seems behind shrewd AA warnings to become alert and HALT when an individual becomes hungry, angry, lonely, or tired. These conditions can count as ego-depleting because they make one emotionally needy and more ready to give in to the desire for alcohol. When vulnerable and hard-pressed, an individual is more in danger of a relapse. The lure of alcohol's effects becomes stronger when you're weakened.

But aren't people always becoming weakened and tired in the course of working and coping with the demands of life? Ego depletion would seem a technical name for a commonly recurring condition. Perhaps so. But ego depletion theory also holds more hopefully that one common way to restore and replenish ego depletion is to participate in positive emotions. Thus, laughing, talking to a friend, or coming upon novel, beautiful, inspiring, or interesting stimuli replenishes depleted energies. All the good things that humans love and delight in can fill and lift the human spirit. Destructive pleasures, such as addictive drinking, provide only temporary and substitute relief that exact other tolls. The pragmatic AA program offers helpful advice and strategies for maintaining self-control when vulnerable: call sponsors and other AA members for supportive conversation or other needs. Being with friends is humanity's greatest support and delight.

This new research on ego depletion may be just beginning, but its suggestions about self-control and positive emotions sound in accord with human experience. AA's remarkable success for those for whom it works may be due in part to the way an addicted alcoholic becomes depleted and exhausted in his losing struggle to manage, control, cover up, deny, or rationalize destructive drinking. To finally give up, acknowledge the truth, and enter a relationship with a Higher Power and a supportive group can produce a flood of replenishing positive emotions. Fellowship, storytelling, altruism, and new vistas of thought provide interest and joy. With increasing and renewing wellsprings of positive feelings opening up within the program, individuals can access the energy to begin the hard work of changing themselves in cooperation with others. Recovery requires achieving self-management and the ability to identify and outwit inner assaults from negative feelings. Emotional wildfires or emotional flooding are destructive. The psychological and spiritual tools that are recommended to help in times of struggle, such as prayer, meditation, and meetings generate positive emotions: Go to meetings, call your sponsor, call other members, pray, read, meditate, do service work. When alone, meditation and prayer focus attention on positive feelings of trust in God and away from anger, resentment, conflict, and sorrows. In AA the fluctuation of negative and positive emotions is recognized. The divided, mixed nature of human consciousness is a recognized fact of life, and never underestimated.

Danger lurks not only when ego depleted but when encountering people, places, and things associated with past abuses of alcohol. Irrational thinking can pop into the mind to justify giving in to the desire for alcohol. Many AA members have dramatically testified to their near-demonic recurrence of cravings for alcohol. "This disease wants me dead," they say. The clever variants of self-deceptive strategies are reported. Often there is some part of a person that does not want to recover or be happy. Man is in love with his suffering, Dostoevsky has a character assert. He goes on to describe those defiant individuals who would rather remain unique and isolated in their suffering, than surrender and be happy with all the others. A crucial part of the process of becoming happy is desiring to become happy. Experiencing positive emotions with others can arouse the desire for and belief in recovery and happiness. The contagious emotions of love, joy, and interest exert their potent attractive power.

Experiencing positive feelings of acceptance and good will with others can produce the most crucial factor of all in the pursuit of happiness: the willingness to be happy and to change. Happiness, as we have seen, is grounded on a good life that at a minimum does no harm. At a maximum, persons cultivate positive virtues and service to others. In order to carry out all the change described above, a person must want to be moral and want to be happy. Here again the positive emotions exercise a magnetic, contagious power. Desire can be inspired and communicated through living with others' joy, interest, and love.

Indeed, with human beings as they are, the desire for moral and spiritual qualities can be contagious. Imitation is innate to humans, especially in rewarding circumstances such as bonded, caring groups that listen to and accept you. Those whom you admire, love, and enjoy, you imitate. The pleasure of good company draws you on. Emotionally supportive groups provide collective moral guideposts for the spiritual journey as well as the healing balm of acceptance. Individuals feeling emotionally good, adopt, appropriate, and incorporate morally good things into their own lives. Good feelings do the good work of change. Happiness comes from positive emotions and increases contagiously.

AA and its principles and practices offer an eighty-year-old spiritual program for the pursuit of happiness that incorporates psychological truths and group dynamics. A more recent approach to becoming happy is found in the secular positive psychology movement. Here, too, the promise is given that you can become happy, or as we will see, at least happier. And as always, comparing cases can be informative as well as intriguing.

Chapter 6

A POSITIVE PSYCHOLOGY GUIDE TO HAPPINESS

One of the latest burgeoning movements in psychology addresses human happiness and how to achieve it. An academically respected positive psychologist, Sonja Lyubomirsky, PhD, has written a popular self-help book with the straightforward title *The How of Happiness: A Scientific Approach to Getting the Life You Want*. It is a big book, but a fast read. She writes in a warm, reader-friendly style and promises that you, the reader, can become happy—if you follow her directions faithfully and with perseverance. Yes. The news is good. New scientific knowledge makes it possible to obtain lasting happiness.

A key element in this how-to program is a midsection of the book providing twelve Happiness-Enhancing Activities; this intriguing and essential section is explored here. But before plunging into this body of practical material, Lyubomirsky prepares the ground by presenting a general discussion of the new psychological field of happiness studies. She also, in the beginning of her book and again at the end, acts as a responsible psychological professional to alert those readers who might be clinically depressed and need more than her program provides. She includes a standard depression questionnaire and gives a comprehensive discussion of depression, how to recognize it, and its causes and treatments. But since her how-to-be-happy program incorporates many aspects of present treatment strategies for depression, it may help those who are depressed and might even be a first step in the right direction.

For those readers who want to become happier than they are, Lyubomirsky—or more informally, Sonja—presents a program of twelve happiness-enhancing exercises and interventions she has created from current research and practice. She recognizes the faddish aspect of the recent explosion of happiness studies rather ruefully. Happiness is indeed a hot topic in the social science community and in popular culture amounts to almost a craze. While Sonja, as a dedicated academic researcher, might want to keep her distance, she wants to correct popularized myths and misinformation with a reliable self-help book that can help people to greater happiness. To that end she intends to provide evidence-based information and trustworthy practices.

Lyubomirsky is careful to situate her text squarely within the new science of happiness that is emerging within the positive psychology movement. As noted in earlier chapters, this psychological movement has appeared in the last decades among a loosely allied group of academically trained psychologists who have been inspired by the conviction that "empowering people to live the most rewarding and happiest lives they can is just as important as psychology's traditional focus on repairing the weaknesses and healing their pathologies." Human flourishing and fulfillment should be as important a goal as remaining fixated on disease, disorder, and the negative side of life.

The founder and undisputed leader of this movement is the academically distinguished research psychologist Martin Seligman. He had enjoyed an outstanding research career in experimental psychology before shifting and expanding his focus to take psychology in a new direction. Seligman has described these developments in many academic and popular publications but perhaps most succinctly and characteristically in his own popular self-help book *Authentic Happiness*. Here he reemphasizes how he came to start a movement that identifies and encourages positive human strengths. The core concern is helping persons and institutions toward human flourishing and happiness. Seligman, like his younger colleague Lyubomirsky, writes in an accessible style; they both provide a lively potpourri of vignettes, self-assessment questionnaires, case studies, descriptive theories, research studies, and personal life experiences.

Martin Seligman and his followers desire to focus upon encouraging human strengths, which he calls by the traditional term "virtues." To define these virtues, Seligman and a colleague empirically collected concepts of virtue and value from different cross-cultural sources; they then correlated them to come up with a common list. Since religion and spirituality are cross-cultural universal practices, he includes spiritual values as a strength, making positive psychologists faith-friendly or spiritually welcoming. Sonja follows this lead and includes a cluster of spiritual exercises in her recommended practices. Positive psychologists in their overt advocacy of values, virtues, and spirituality have been willing to move beyond established basic science canons of value-free experimental psychology. They adopt the goal of espousing virtues and other good qualities and capacities to modern life and helping people to become happy. Seligman self-confidently does not hesitate to provide his list of central virtues, to affirm virtue's relation to authentic happiness, and to discuss the roles of meaning, love, and purpose in life. He also gives instruction on how to raise children by providing examples from personal experiences.

Naturally philosophers, theologians, and other academic psychologists do not easily countenance positive psychology's free-flowing treatments of complex concepts, but Martin Seligman pushes on. And why not? As a leading American psychologist venturing into new interdisciplinary territory, his arguments deserve a respectful hearing and response. Like Lyubomirsky or any other author he is entitled to present his psychologically informed convictions on important interdisciplinary subjects.

Skeptical critics might note that Seligman and Lyubomirsky, and others of their colleagues, claim the name and aura of science but are less successful in providing the game. Seligman's guidebook on happiness and Sonja's "evidence-based" how-to book continually refer to recent scientific research but spend little time discussing the scientific value of a cited study, or how these scatterings of studies relate to each other or to a coherent theoretical framework. Readers are treated to the constant refrain of "one study found" or "scientific research shows" with no broader or deeper treatment of the complexities of the scientific enterprise. Yet science consists of diverse methodologies, conflicting theoretical foundations, necessary limitations, and notorious difficulties in obtaining reliability and validity. Invocations of the sacred name of science seem to be used more as a rhetorical tool to persuade doubtful readers that they should have faith in the author's message. Trust us, follow our directions, and you, too, can become happy.

Positive psychologists are not actually engaged in a basic scientific enterprise like physics but rather in a wide-ranging, value-laden, reasoned effort to effect social and individual change and solve problems. It would be more forthright to admit that a physical science model is impossible when dealing with self-conscious human agents capable of intentional activities and thoughts. Consciousness and self-consciousness are always factors in human therapeutic efforts to change people. Psychotherapy, education, or even medical treatment programs are more akin to artful persuasion than objective scientific research. A supposedly scientific happiness intervention is more like an educational training course or an effective act of persuasion and conversion than a controlled experiment. Even the positive psychology research tools appearing in the self-help books—like Lyubomirsky's self-report measures, assessment scales, and questionnaires—have their weaknesses as research measures. Therapeutic self-help happiness interventions can be better appreciated as valuable efforts to persuade and educate people to adopt those moral, reasonable, and virtuous thoughts and behaviors that will bring them happiness. Perhaps the new descriptions appearing of these interventions as "life coaching" is a more accurate label. A life coach, like an educator, is not a scientist or even a psychotherapist modeled on a medical doctor. Yet these coaching and therapeutic educational efforts can be beneficial when they are in accord with rationally grounded moral worldviews and accrued psychological and cultural wisdom.

Humanistic and religious thinkers recognize the truth that science is only one path to knowledge and only one valuable way of being rational and reasonable. Who could make all of life's decisions based solely on reliable scientific findings? For one thing, consistently verifiable scientific data are too sparse; for another, new theories and discoveries constantly change the rules and content for what is scientifically valid. Consequently those positive psychologists and happiness researchers who are pioneering new interdisciplinary humanistic territory and practical interventions can be encouraged. Their innovations may prove fruitful. Even new media interventions and happiness programs and life coaching on the Internet, like Happier.com, may be of value for some persons. The test will be found in the fruits of these efforts. As long as financial scams, power trips, or exploitation of vulnerable people are not involved, then people can try new things. A science-supporting psychologist and convinced Christian like myself can readily affirm that complex realities and powers exist beyond available empirical proof and can produce healing effects. Think of the new scientific research on the puzzling operations of placebos in medicine. More to the point in the happiness pursuit, remember that the AA movement brings healing and a new happiness without yet being explained by science. A healing practice can be rational, reasonable, principled, and wise, but not explained by empirical scientific research. To inform, educate, coach, persuade, and inspire individuals to adopt positive values (either explicitly or implicitly) is a worthwhile undertaking.

Sonja Lyubomirsky introduces the central role of virtuous values right at the start of her how-to book. She firmly states that an individual's success depends upon commitment to the hard work that the program entails. Perseverance is needed if the happiness-enhancing activities are to operate successfully. Although initially the exercises and practices prescribed may seem off-putting, or "hokey," they work when persistently practiced long enough. Altering ingrained habits and initiating new ones is a difficult task that takes effort and skilled application. The person seeking greater happiness should conscientiously complete the proferred diagnostic questionnaires as well as follow through on the relevant happiness-enhancing exercises.

Lasting happiness is not achieved in a day, or without hard work. An individual has to muster the personal commitment to succeed because no one can take responsibility for another person's inner life. No one can be happy for someone else. But how is the goal of happiness to be recognized and defined? Happiness, for Lyubomirsky, is "the experience of joy and contentment, or positive well-being, combined with a sense that one's life is good, meaningful, and worthwhile." This description is concise and comprehensive; it integrates the experiential, subjective, emotional feeling of happiness with the more thoughtful satisfactions and contentments of human flourishing. As discussed in chapter 2 of this volume, the two dimensions of emotion and thought regularly appear in efforts to define happiness. When people jokingly say that they know happiness when they see or feel it, a bit of probing produces concepts of happiness that include positive pleasurable emotion and some sense of a positively existing, estimated good value. Lyubomirsky's inclusive description of happiness captures these different dimensions. She goes on to assert that different elements of happiness may appear in complexly different kinds and amounts. You can feel happy in many ways, with different patterns and in different ranges of intensity.

Lyubomirsky's introductory discussion of happiness includes a theory that assigns causes and individual characteristics to personal happiness. She follows other positive psychologists in their claim that we should think of an individual's happiness as a circular pie graph that is divided, like Gaul, into three parts. Fifty percent of the pie is determined by our genetic inheritance that produces an individual's set point, or inherited temperamental level of potential happiness. This set point is thought to be more or less a permanent value that does not change over time. Ten percent of the pie comes from changing external circumstances that a person cannot control, but 40 percent is caused by intentional activity or individual agency. The 40 percent of the pie that can be changed and controlled presents the greatest challenge for happiness psychologists like Lyubomirsky. Because 40 percent is almost half of one's whole state of being, individuals can construct and control their general happiness through their intentional thoughts, actions, and attitudes. Thus, the exuberant claim that our happiness "is entirely in our hands"—or almost entirely: almost half is ours to determine.

Critics of these claims can have serious reservations and mount counterarguments. Does a quantitative approach employing the static graphic symbol of a divided pie make sense when dealing with the dynamic, qualitative flow of human streams of consciousness? Consciousness rises and falls in quicksilver movements moving from positive to negative responses and complex mixtures of the two not easily captured by a graph. Is it ever possible to successfully divide or separate genetic factors from environmental circumstances or for that matter easily separate intentional actions from the environment? Human brains are continually immersed in social environments where they are receiving and processing stimuli that they must interpret; their constructs can become their environment. However, if these objections to an oversimplistic pie graph approach can be put aside, the theory makes a valuable heuristic point: human beings actively create their lives as well as being created by them. While inherited temperament can be a factor, unimpaired adults can make intentional choices and be guided by self-reflective conscious and rational goals. Beyond survival levels and unusual emergency conditions, happiness need not be solely dependent upon social status, material possessions, good looks, inherited talent, or other turns of the wheel of fortune. Here indeed, empirical descriptive research has found that neither unexpected catastrophes nor strokes of good luck permanently determine subjective well-being or levels of happiness. A person's response to what happens to him or her can be as important as what is happening.

This encouraging emphasis upon the power of inner self-agency, will, and conscious causation is to be highly valued as the generator of virtues and human strengths, but it seems somewhat at odds with the assertion that 50 percent of individual happiness is determined by the genes, producing a "set point" or limited potential for happiness. Is this really so? Positive personal transformations of character and temperament are frequently encountered. Individuals undergo religious conversions or become emotionally and behaviorally transformed in AA programs. Other people are radically changed through intense psychotherapy, or change mentally, emotionally, and physically through prolonged meditation. While identical twin studies have provided evidence for genetic influences on personality, a lot of burgeoning attention is also being paid to ongoing environmental control of gene expression. The workings of human genetic inheritance and interactions remain a vast, unknown territory. As more becomes known about individual powers of emotional regulation, consciousness control, and other intervention programs, individuals may well come to be seen as less genetically determined than heretofore thought. The concept of genetic set points in happiness interventions might be better laid to rest.

Another problematic theoretical assertion in the happiness literature also relates to the idea of limitations—the idea of the hedonic treadmill. The concept asserts that happiness interventions are fated to be temporary because adaptation to a condition automatically induces ever-increasing need for more stimulation or satisfaction—just to stay at the same place. Individuals on their hedonic treadmill find it hard to be happy for long where they happen to be. Once adapted to a new level of happiness, old stimuli are no longer experienced with the same positive pleasure, so dissatisfaction, restlessness, and boredom constantly spur on individuals. Certainly the human capacity for adaptation to stimuli is a part of human life. Admittedly, too, in modern capitalistic societies, advertisers and businesses encourage consumers to quickly adapt to the new so that they can buy and consume more toys and products at an ever greater pace.

But human beings always and everywhere become deeply attached to familiar faces and places, to customary routines and rituals, and to ideas current in their known worlds. Individuals take pleasure and find contentment in familiar individuals, known landscapes, and repeated routines. Pleasures and happiness arise from reassuring sameness. Persons seem to take as much joy in the familiar as in the novel. In happiness intervention programs, as in daily life, deactivating dissatisfying hedonic treadmills or the lust for the new and different may be fairly easy. As noted in Lyubomirsky's happiness-enhancing exercises, living fully and savoring the present is an important habit that must be learned. Here and now is where one cultivates the happiness-making attitudes of being grateful, savoring present goods, and nurturing existing relationships. Present-oriented strategies work toward increasing happiness and moving attention away from a future need for more input that is different and distant. These strategies are also seen in AA's spiritual program, where a sober person learns to live gratefully and serenely in the present moment—one day at a time.

In fact, as has been discussed previously and again below, new research on positive emotions such as joy and happiness can engender more present happiness in upward spirals and building and broadening responses. So, perhaps, as Sonja notes later in her book, some estimates of the successes of people permanently obtaining their positive goals on their own may be too low. The case for happiness may actually be a better one than certain pessimistic theories predict. Examining Lyubomirsky's twelve happiness-enhancing exercises may also be useful for general application or to confirm other understandings of happiness.

The Twelve Happiness-Enhancing Exercises

To ensure the highest chances of success in her intervention program, Lyubomirsky wants to induce a good match between individuals and the specific exercises they attempt. Her rationale is that since individuals vary, and different kinds of happiness and reliable happiness activities exist, a goodness of fit between individual and method is important. To achieve this fit, Sonja provides a preliminary diagnostic questionnaire keyed to the twelve exercises. An individual is directed to fill out the questionnaire with care and score it properly. The scoring shows which three or four happiness-enhancing activities of the twelve will be best suited for that particular person. The diagnostic test asks an individual to give an assessment of activities as being "enjoyable" or "natural" and which would be done out of "duty," "guilt," or "social coercion." Those activities that are seen as enjoyable or natural should be chosen since they will be more likely to succeed, and those assessed as likely to be followed only out of "duty," "guilt," or "social coercion" put aside as less likely to succeed. An activity that is reluctantly performed is less likely to be practiced over a long enough period to become a new habit. If, however, the new happiness activities tap into "genuine interests and deeply held values," then doing them will become easier. With repetition, the activities themselves produce a self-determined motivation because you will be happier as you do them. The proof will be in the pudding. Progress in the program is assessed by retaking the standard happiness questionnaire that is provided and measuring your improved score.

If the initially chosen strategies don't work after a conscientious effort, then your personal commitment to happiness is tested by your willingness to reassess, readjust, and try other exercises of the twelve activities provided. Again and again, Lyubomirsky encourages her readers to persevere by reiterating the message that it is truly possible to gain lasting happiness. Indeed, it is the "most rewarding work you'll ever do." Taking the various questionnaires, practicing the exercises, thinking about the various aspects in your life—all of these are promised to open new vistas and be transformative. Sonja in a personal afterword claims that she herself was changed for the better by writing the book. It made her venture more deeply into the various happiness activities, and she found that those that were less natural to her, such as spirituality, benefited her the most. Perhaps this comment may cast some doubt on Martin Seligman's theory that people should always go with, focus upon, or cultivate their signature strengths rather than their other personal characteristics. Such unresolved questions about the psychology of happiness arise frequently in this relatively new field. They surface and are discussed in more depth in Lyubomirsky's later section on why the program works, or the secrets of the program. But before grappling with these intriguing theoretical questions, we should skim some of the specifics of the twelve happiness-enhancing exercises. Everyone also can read the book for the detailed presentations, complete with questionnaires and vignettes.

The number of happiness exercises provided actually adds up to more than twelve, because under each heading so many subsets of related activities and admonitions are nested together. One general impression of this array is that it comes off as a gourmet cookbook or a software manual. More accurately and to the point, the reader can find here a reprise of all the good advice and wise lessons you would learn while growing up in a good home, a cohesive neighborhood, and a benign religious community. If you were brought up in a good family, received an adequate education and a sound moral and religious formation, then you have encountered these twelve civilizing exercises—although probably not in the language of psychology. These exercises are a crash course or compendium of the prudential and virtuous traditions of civilized culture, full of common sense, morality, and rules of responsible self-management: Be grateful, optimistic, kind, forgiving, spiritual, generous, prudent, responsible, and so forth.

Appropriately enough, at the headings of the twelve different treatments are relevant quotes from great literary and religious figures that set the tone for the advice. Apt sayings from Emerson, George Eliot, and Robert Louis Stevenson are cited, along with the Talmud, St. Francis de Sales, and Saint Paul's Epistle to the Romans. Here again, including wisdom from many sources with generic, virtuously spiritual elements provides a similarity to AA's program. The twelve happiness exercises, like the twelve AA steps, are eclectic and presented in a number of loosely related clusters. The exercises, however, include copious references to psychological knowledge and research. One psychological cluster of exercises, the number-three mandates to avoid "overthinking and social comparisons," are based upon cognitive behavior therapy and research. This focus on self-regulating patterns in thinking emerges from research which finds that excessive rumination and self-conscious criticisms can lead to depression. Other exercises in this psychological self-management cluster give advice on ways to cope with stress, choose commitments, and take care of your needs for physical activity. The psychological understanding that certain ways of acting produce the requisite emotions—number twelve's "Act like a happy person"—is based on emotion research as well as cognitive behavior therapy. The body-mind unity of human beings ensures that bodily actions can influence emotional feelings as well as the other way round.

These ideas are quite familiar to many people from childhood. As well-brought-up southern girls, heirs to generations of southern Protestant piety, my sister and I were regularly subjected to Pollyanna, "the glad girl," books. She had learned to put on a smile, act glad, be generous, always see the best of everything, and so find her way to happiness and success. My family had never heard of positive cognitive behavior therapy, much less of AA's slogans, such as "Fake it 'til you make it," or "Move a muscle, change a thought." But the same lessons were clearly given: Don't mope around feeling sorry for yourself, look on the bright side, make the best of it, don't hold grudges, show some backbone, and get up and go, finish what you start. And so on and so on, until you achieve a good, honorable character and kind, gracious manners. We did not encounter that latter-day heroine of *The Little Engine That Could*, but we understood that "I think I can, I think I can" was the way to live. How reinforcing it is to find as an adult that an American can-do childhood garners research support from positive psychology! Indeed, optimistic thinking makes sense philosophically as well as psychologically for those who believe that we live within an open future that is not fatalistically foreclosed. The complex possibility of various future outcomes leaves room for effective personal agency energized by positive attitudes.

Research in positive psychology also supports other traditional self-management strategies incorporated into the happiness exercises. Lyubomirsky's number eight urges getting intensely involved in absorbing activities and finding flow states. In flow you give yourself over to absorbing tasks and activities and lose those nagging self-conscious tendencies to self-criticism. The self enlarges and expands as it becomes given over to activities, and individuals find themselves refreshed and happy. In much the same process, cultivating and nurturing social relationships (number five) is another reliable strategy for turning attention away from the isolated self. Individuals become enhanced by engaging in satisfying give-and-take with others. The strategic need to turn outward to positive relations *with* others blends into happiness exercises for pursuing activities *for* others. In nurturing others, you gain altruistic satisfactions from giving and loving as well as from social stimulation.

A central cluster of Sonja's happiness exercises are spiritually oriented in that they consist of moral and religious mandates and admonitions. These exercises advise individuals to be grateful, to be kind, to forgive others, to savor and appreciate the good things of life, and to practice spirituality, religion, and meditation. Here one finds the faith-friendly characteristics of positive psychology. Rationales for this spiritual turn in "scientific" psychology are that research shows overwhelmingly that happy people are found to be religious, grateful, kind, forgiving, savoring the good, and practicing prayer or meditation. Although Sonja can say of herself that she is the least spiritual person of all, she does a good job describing the positive effects of spiritual and religious beliefs and practices. The requisite warning appears against unbalanced toxic varieties of religion, but on the whole Lyubomirsky gives a favorable appraisal of the way religion gives meaning, comfort, and above all, social support in its beliefs and practices.

Lyubomirsky recognizes that it is beyond psychology's capacity to empirically research the actual truths of religious claims. But psychology can empirically investigate what effects religious faith and spiritual practices have on those who do believe. The positive findings on the health, happiness, and flourishing of religious believers and altruists is a factor in the new openness of psychology to religious faith and spirituality. An older default dogmatic atheism has receded, although personally many psychological investigators like Sonja remain unbelievers. However, as a humanist sensitive to moral and aesthetic values, Lyubomirsky speaks of our human ability to create and bestow meaningful sacredness upon the ordinary experiences of living and loving. In her worldview, however, sanctifying or making sacred is a purely human activity. There is no transcendent loving God or Higher Power as in AA, initiating, attracting, or cooperatively engendering human spiritual experiences. There is only an I and no Thou.

Perhaps this is one characteristic of positive psychology's approach to happiness. All is done on the horizontal human level according to secular reality. There's no imagined vision of a God perspective or divine truth. Everything—even meditation, prayer, and sanctifying efforts—are measured and evaluated by whether it makes us happy or not. Transcendent truth, reality, and unconditioned love are by-passed. We are told to forgive others not because a loving God has forgiven us but because it will make us happier and healthier. Religion is recommended not because it is true but because 95 percent of people believe, and it can be good for you. As exercise number eleven, practicing religion and spirituality, sums it up, "If you so choose, and in your own way, you can harness the benefits of faith to improve your happiness and your life." The critical objection that springs to mind is whether a human whose goal is to "harness" the benefits of faith can actually do so. The standard distinction between "intrinsic" and "extrinsic" religion casts doubts on the transformative power of extrinsic religious practice.

In any event, in Lyubomirsky's individual-centered program, persons can freely choose which effective happiness exercises will work for them. Apparently an ardent unbeliever or devout atheist could simply avoid the spiritual clusters of the strategies offered. Here is another interesting contrast with AA. Individual freedom to choose activities is stressed in both programs, but in AA there is a required core curriculum: the spiritual acceptance of a transcendent, benign Higher Power and a mandatory service of others—although a single interpretation of what this entails is not necessary. There is more unity in AA. It would be interesting to know whether there is any necessary distribution requirement in Sonja's program to achieve happiness. Could you avoid all the spiritual and moral aspects of the clusters if that is your preference? It would be crucial to know if the private psychological self-management practices would suffice. Perhaps it would depend upon how unhappy or happy you were to begin with and how much you already informally or implicitly incorporate other exercises.

Those embarking on the AA program recognize that they are desperately unhappy in lives that are unmanageable. Their clear need for help makes them ready to accept the unified and prescribed twelve-step spirituality to achieve sobriety and the promise of a new happiness. Admitting their dependence upon a Higher Power is primary and essential to begin their journey. Later steps recommend regular prayer and meditation and come after required acts of repentance, confession, reparation, forgiveness, and service. By contrast, Lyubomirsky's program allows so much choice that one could theoretically skip forgiveness or kindness. While it is recognized that AA's dependence, repentance, forgiveness, service, prayer, and meditation are going to benefit the individuals themselves by bringing them happiness, AA maintains a focus upon God or a real Higher Power that exists as other and beyond. The alcoholic learns that he must conform to God's reality in order for the self to be given the power to achieve happiness. An individual embarking on Lyubomirsky's happiness activities is by contrast employing or "harnessing" human psychological powers to become happy. AA gives a vision of a transcendent power within and beyond toward which one journeys as a joyful pilgrim; positive psychology provides the seeker access to inside expertise and broad knowledge.

Both programs demand hard work, commitment, and willingness to learn new ways of thinking, feeling, and acting. No one can change and grow without embracing new disciplines of practice, practice, practice. Both programs use the ancient magic number twelve to arbitrarily divide a multitude of interrelated life lessons written in accessible (often hokey) language. And both draw on some of the same deep psychological powers or "secrets" of transforming processes. Sonja's section on the secrets of why the program works presents what she thinks are "the five hows behind sustainable happiness." These core psychological ingredients overlap with the features that I think are central to AA's effectiveness—with some key differences.

The Secrets or Five Hows behind Sustainable Happiness

Sonja Lyubomirsky claims that five essential psychological ingredients make her program for achieving sustainable happiness succeed. They are "Positive Emotion," "Optimal Timing and Variety," "Social Support," "Motivation, Effort and Commitment," and "Habit." To start with the last and work backward, it is easy to see that changing habits is essential. Self-destructive habits make us miserable, and achieving good habits bring, happiness. Positive physical habits produce healthy bodies, and positive mental and emotional habits help us become happy through feelings of gratitude, kindness, nurturing, forgiveness, optimistic thinking, and spiritual practice. The less well known news that positive psychology asserts is that new and better habits can be rather readily formed through repeated intentional efforts. Humans are malleable, flexible, and ever-changing; they are able to be conditioned and to condition themselves.

The optimism of positive psychology's message is partly based upon human abilities to learn new things and the fact that humans have the strength and willpower to freely choose some acts of behavior. This strength of human agency makes virtue and growth possible. Conscious voluntary effort can create personal change if a person is committed to working hard and given the tools to do so. Self-efficacy is innate to human nature, and individuals can work hard to achieve future goals. Sonja's how of motivation, commitment, and effort to achieve a goal is an innate ability of human beings displayed from infancy to old age. Repeated voluntary actions can create virtuous new habits, and new habitual responses add up to a changed personality.

AA also asserts that individuals can make decisions and can do so repeatedly with the support of God and the group in order to change their habits. Negative entrapping habits are also explicitly recognized and given their due as obstacles in AA. However, if you backslide—or, in AA language, "relapse," "pick up," or "go out of the rooms"—you can always begin again and persevere one day at a time until you "get it." As in the classic story of Robert Bruce, who was inspired to continue his military campaign by a spider's repeated efforts to anchor her web, the spider never gave up her efforts to anchor her web until she succeeded. Positive psychology is on the side of the spider. And so is AA's Higher Power.

Sonja gives full weight to the familiar factor of motivation and commitment, but she thinks that another, less well known "secret" of self-change lies in the timing of efforts. Dogged repetition is necessary, but variety is the spice of life. Optimal timing and spontaneously trying new ways to practice the exercises can achieve the balance to help sustain positive responses. It is a shrewd self-management move to know the optimal time to schedule an exercise. As in a diet or physical exercise program, the aim is not to become so rigid that boredom, rebellion, or revulsion set in. Sonja cites religious liturgical practice as a good example of how varied rituals and seasonal changes make "clever use of optimal timing" to sustain continuity and commitment. AA also provides variety amid continuity through scheduling different kinds of meetings and celebrations with different group readings from the standard texts. Invariably, too, supportive stimulation comes from the variety of unpredictable personal interchanges in meetings. Face-to-face interactions with others help achieve and sustain change.

Social support is another of the five secrets that Sonja gives for how happiness-enhancement exercises work. She singles out AA's capacity to provide "galvanizing commitment" through the power of peers sharing experiences in face-to-face meetings. Indeed, the power of group influence in AA is primary. Lyubomirsky recognizes this need for social support to effect change but can only recommend finding it and hoping that one does. This seems a major weakness of a how-to-be-happy program given through the medium of printed instructions. Reading is a private, individualized, distancing form of communication. Can it work by itself without a group to galvanize commitment—or, for that matter, to interpret the words and questionnaires without self-serving distortions? The text can tell you to go get social support but can't guarantee it will happen. The emotional dynamics that take place in a face-to-face relationship may be crucially important for emotional change. Traditional psychodynamic therapies and new affective interpersonal therapies assert that the emotions present in the immediate interpersonal relationship effect real change. It would seem a large order to bring to bear from a text imagined representations that have the same power that focused interpersonal relationships do.

Without an interpersonal group relationship, another of AA's how or transforming effects is blocked: the group's construction of a personal narrative that builds a new identity. Constructing and telling one's story over and over, and having a supportive group as an audience, helps create and nurture the new person. The positive emotional validation creates the new happiness while simultaneously directly increasing it. In a way, with Lyubomirsky's program of activities the seeker of happiness has to play all the parts solo. You take the questionnaires, score them, choose the preferred strategies, decide whether they need readjustment, keep motivating yourself, and vigilantly sustain the various self-management strategies. While the program tells you to get out of yourself in order to be happy, the individual-centered, self-focused monitoring works against it. While being advised to "avoid overthinking" the efforts at self-management, self-care, and self-measurement of achieved happiness endanger the enterprise. Am I happier now; will my score on the happiness questionnaire be higher? There can be no turning yourself over to receive God's gifts of power to help inspire or carry you along in the supportive company of other pilgrims. But perhaps the primary secret power of positive emotion can do the job.

Positive emotion is the number-one how of Sonja's program, and in my judgment appropriately so. She heads the discussion with a quote from Benjamin Franklin (that great positive psychologist?). "Happiness," he says, "consists more in small conveniences or pleasures that occur every day, than in great pieces of good fortune that happen but seldom." As long as those pleasures are of the moral quality that bring satisfaction and contentment he is correct, since we must live in the present moment. Lyubomirsky affirms that all twelve of her activities work because they produce positive emotional "feelings of joy, delight, contentment, serenity, curiosity, interest, vitality, enthusiasm, vigor, thrill, and pride," and these are the "very hallmark of happiness." Indeed, she states, "Positive emotions make happy people who they are."

These experiences of positive emotion, as in the AA spiritual program, do not mean that happy people don't suffer or feel pain and sorrow. Life is difficult, and we share sorrows with others when we live empathetically and altruistically. Happy people are deeply engaged with others, nurturing relationships, being kind, engaging in service, or choosing virtuous behaviors like forgiving or spirituality. But as repeatedly stressed in the new understandings of emotion and the complexity of human consciousness, it is possible to feel deep and abiding joy at the same time as passing pains or suffering. Empathetic suffering positively engages and enlarges a person's ability to experience joy and happiness in a way that resentment or negative emotions cannot.

Positive emotions, as we now know, broaden our attention, build up activities, and can even undo past traumatic experiences. Positive emotions may come in small boosts or lifting of spirits, but they build and become positive habits of the heart. Savoring and being grateful for the everyday moments of life change who we are. Sonja gives a long quote from Proust describing how his exquisite pleasure in the taste of the Madeleine in his tea was able to inspire feelings of love and hope in life. The important point to be made is that positive feelings of emotion and pleasure work *for* and *with* the meaningful and moral values of human life. The suspicion against joy and happiness as dangerous to the higher life of grim duty is misplaced. Destructive sinful or immoral pleasures can exist, but they come with a painful price that is usually obvious. Positive emotions compatible with love and virtue feel good and are judged to be good; they build up personal and social bonding. These moments of happiness create good lives.

Can the positive emotions innate to human beings operate with enough power to overcome the individualistic, self-focusing orientation that a person undertaking Lyubomirsky's program might choose from the twelve activities? Or as other believers might worry, can a generic, nondefined "spirituality" effectively help persons get in touch with liberating currents of reality beyond self-created illusions? Similar questions arise with AA's twelve-step spiritual program. My answer after much reflection is that positive emotions are so important, so innate, and so potent that they can give birth to human happiness without explicit acknowledgments of the presence of God's grace. It might be more possible to create a self-enclosed pseudo-happy state by choosing only Lyubomirsky's self-management strategies and exercises, but not likely. Sonja's program also lacks the person-to-person corrections and validations of actual other people, but if one follows through on the outward social engagement thrust of the exercises, the danger of verbal-only reality could be avoided as well.

My other corroborating examples are twofold. Reading a sex manual and reading a how-to-give-birth labor guide are printed texts, with or without pictures. Even if valid facts and information are presented, reading a printed text is a far cry from actually having sex or birthing a baby. However, the innate human processes once initiated in everyday life will produce a powerful trajectory that can take over and produce a new reality. In the same way, embarking upon the happiness exercises (however hokey and off-putting) of Sonja's how-to-be-happy program can initiate or release potent innate predispositions producing positive emotions. Positive emotions build upon themselves and increase ten-fold. The psychological research findings on emotional and cognitive behavior processes that are cited to encourage faith in these exercises do not produce certainty, but they do produce increased probabilities of effectiveness. With all of the above caveats, Lyubomirsky's program along with its theoretical base in positive psychology can be seen as a way to become happy. Certainly AA can produce its testimonies from personal experience, so these two case studies provide hope.

Chapter 7

HAPPINESS IN THE FUTURE

Happiness is forever, as Christians believe. In our twenty-first-century present, the perennial human pursuit of happiness has taken off with a record crew and an expansive flight plan. Scientists have entered the pilots' cabin, and more passengers than ever have signed up for the trip. Will the flight be as successful as promised? Pessimists predict that this trip to Utopia is doomed to crash and burn, but I argue that they are wrong. The flight may be bumpy, but it will never be turned back to its point of origin and be cancelled.

As a traveler on this most recent quest for happiness, my goal has been to confront core controversial questions and make a case for my answers. Yes, human happiness is a reality that comes from God and can be successfully pursued here and now. Yes, individuals can become happy, and they and the world will be better for it. These core affirmations, much elaborated and argued for here, are such complicated issues that they will demand decades more research and work. Be prepared; many, many more books, studies, and research projects on all facets of happiness are on their way. We hear only the opening bars of the overture of a very long symphony consisting of many movements.

The movement to create and address a new politics of happiness will slowly work its way to the center of a global society facing more crises and revolutionary unrest. The theme of the individual's pursuit of happiness will swell to ever greater proportion. Confrontations within and between science and religion will have to be addressed more fully.

Pessimists in all camps will insist on a closer examination of the dark side of humanity's failures, sins, and conditions of suffering. Whence do the obstacles and resistances to happiness and the good come from, if not from human hearts of darkness? Resistance to the pursuit of happiness and obstacles in its path must be analyzed fearlessly and honestly.

In the near future, more attention and analysis will be needed to compare the different spiritual and theological paths to happiness that now exist. A comparison of Christian and Buddhist spiritual practices can be welcomed as Buddhism in America attracts more followers, including some who claim to remain Christian. Are the obstacles to growth toward happiness envisioned differently?

Scientifically and psychologically, the biggest questions will turn on further analysis of individual freedom to desire, will, believe, choose, and persevere in answering the call to happiness. The most pressing need for psychology and science is to understand human consciousness; this need may ultimately be more critical than understanding the fate of the cosmos. The inner moral questions of consciousness that are so intimately and undeniably entwined with the pursuit of happiness cannot be bracketed when it expands in scope.

Certainly, our secular and psychological age can be counted on to continue to invest its hope and resources in science. But it seems a less certain bet whether religion and theology possess enough authority to cope with the questions that must be addressed. Will it come to pass in the near future that God's authorship of the drama of human happiness will receive its rightful thanks and praise? I devoutly hope so.

NOTES AND SAMPLES OF SOURCES

A full bibliography on happiness studies would extend three or four times the length of the text. However, it may be helpful to sample a few of the different kinds of sources. Below are (1) some general historical and intellectual discussions, (2) a selection of popular guide books, and (3) examples of more specialized psychological and scientific articles.

General Historical and Intellectual Discussions
on Happiness, Emotions, and the Adaptive Unconscious

Bok, Derek. *The Politics of Happiness: What Government Can Learn from the New Research on Well Being.* Princeton, NJ: Princeton University Press, 2010.

Bok, Sissela. *Exploring Happiness: From Aristotle to Brain Science.* New Haven, CT: Yale University Press, 2010.

Bloom, Paul. "The Moral Life of Babies." *The New York Times Magazine*, May 9, 2010.

Callahan, Sidney. *Created for Joy: A Christian View of Suffering.* New York: Crossroad, 2007.

——. *In Good Conscience: Reason and Emotion in Moral Decision Making.* San Francisco: HarperSanFrancisco, 1991.

——. "The Psychology of Emotion and the Ethics of Care." In *Medicine and the Ethics of Care.* Edited by Diana Fritz Cates and Paul Lauritzen, 141-61. Washington DC: Georgetown University Press, 2001.

——. *Women Who Hear Voices: The Challenge of Religious Experience.* Mahwah, NJ: Paulist Press, 2003.

Csikszentimihalyi. Mihalyi. *Flow: The Psychology of Optimal Experience.* New York: Harper & Row, 1990.

Dalai Lama, The, and H. C. Cutler. *The Art of Happiness: A Handbook of Living.* New York: Riverhead Books, 1998.

Damasio, Antonio. *Descartes' Error: Emotion, Reason, and the Human Brain.* New York: Putnam, 1994.

Doidge, Norman. *The Brain That Changes Itself: Stories of Personal Triumph from the Frontiers of Brain Science.* New York: Viking, 2007.

Gilbert, Daniel. *Stumbling on Happiness*. New York: Alfred A. Knopf, 2006.

Gladwell, Malcolm. *Blink: The Power of Thinking without Thinking*. New York: Little, Brown and Company, 2005.

Glover, Jonathan. *Humanity: A Moral History of the Twentieth Century*. New Haven, CT: Yale University Press, 1999.

Goleman, Daniel. *Emotional Intelligence*. New York: W. W. Norton, 1995.

Gopnik, Alison. *The Philosophical Baby: What Children's Minds Tell Us about Truth, Love, and the Meaning of Life*. New York. Farrar, Straus and Giroux, 2009.

Haidt, Jonathan. *The Happiness Hypothesis: Finding Modern Truth in Ancient Wisdom*. New York: Basic Books, 2006.

Hoffman, Eva. *After Such Knowledge: Memory, History, and the Legacy of the Holocaust*. New York: Public Affairs, 2004.

Jamison, Kay Redfield. *Exuberance: The Passion for Life*. New York: Vintage Books, 2005.

Kingwell, Mark. *In Pursuit of Happiness: Better Living from Plato to Prozac*. New York: Crown Publishers, 1998.

McMahon, Darrin M. *Happiness: A History*. New York: Atlantic Monthly Press, 2006.

Murphy, Nancey. *Bodies and Souls, or Spirited Bodies?* Cambridge: Cambridge University Press, 2006.

Myers, David G. *The Pursuit of Happiness: Discovering the Pathway to Fulfillment, Well-Being, and Enduring Personal Joy*. New York: HarperCollins, 1992.

Nettle, Daniel. *Happiness: The Science behind Your Smile*. Oxford: Oxford University Press, 2005.

Pinker, Stephen. *How the Mind Works*. New York: W.W. Norton, 1997.

Stark, Rodney. *The Rise of Christianity: A Sociologist Reconsiders History*. Princeton, NJ: Princeton University Press, 1996.

——. *The Victory of Reason: How Christianity Led to Freedom, Capitalism, and Western Success*. New York: Random House, 2005.

Toner, Jules. *Love and Friendship*. Milwaukee: Marquette University Press, 2003.

White, Nicholas. *A Brief History of Happiness*. Oxford: Blackwell, 2006.

Wilson, David Sloan. *Darwin's Cathedral: Evolution, Religion and the Nature of Society*. Chicago: University of Chicago Press, 2002.

Wilson, Timothy D. *Strangers to Ourselves: Discovering the Adaptive Unconscious*. Cambridge, MA: Harvard University Press, 2002.

Popular Guide Books

Ben-Shahar, Ben. *Happier: Learn the Secret to Daily Joy and Lasting Fulfillment*. New York: McGraw Hill, 2007.

Diener, Ed, and Robert Biswas-Diener. *Happiness: Unlocking the Mysteries of Psychological Wealth*. Oxford: Blackwell, 2008.

Lyubomirsky, Sonja. *The How of Happiness: A Scientific Approach to Getting the Life You Want.* New York: Penguin Press, 2007.

Salzberg, Sharon. *LovingKindness: The Revolutionary Art of Happiness.* Boston and London: Shambhala, 2002.

Seligman, Martin E. P. *Authentic Happiness: Using the New Positive Psychology to Realize Your Potential for Lasting Fulfillment.* New York: Free Press, 2002.

Specialized Psychological and Scientific Sources

American Psychologist. Special Issue on Happiness, Excellence and Optimal Human Functioning, 55, no. 1 (January 2000).

Black, David M, ed. *Psychoanalysis and Religion in the 21st Century: Competitors or Collaborators?* London and New York: Routledge, 2006.

Cacioppo, J. T., and G. G. Bernston. "The Affect System Has Parallel and Integrative Processing Components: Form Follows Function." *Journal of Personality and Social Psychology* 76, no. 5 (1999): 839–55.

——, and W. L. Gardner. *Emotion: Annual Review of Psychology* 50 (1999): 191–214.

Carstensen, L. L., H. L. Fung, and S. T. Charles. "Socioemotional Selectivity Theory and Emotion Regulation in the Second Half of Life." *Motivation and Emotion* 27, no. 2 (June 2003): 103–23.

Custers, Ruud, and Henk Aarts. "Positive Affect as Implicit Motivator: On the Nonconscious Operation of Behavioral Goals." *Journal of Personality and Social Psychology* 89, no. 2 (August 2005): 129–42.

Diener, Ed, Richard E. Lucas, and Christie Napa Scollon. "Beyond the Hedonic Treadmill: Revising the Adaptation Theory of Well-Being." *American Psychologist* 61, no 4 (2006): 305–14.

Ekman, Paul. "Facial Expression and Emotion." *American Psychologist* 48, no. 4 (April 1993): 384–92.

Feldman Barrett, Lisa, Paula M. Niedenthal, and Piotr Winkielman, eds. *Emotion and Consciousness.* New York: Guilford Press, 2005.

——, and James A. Russell. "Independence and Bipolarity in the Structure of Affect." *Journal of Personality and Social Psychology* 74, no. 4 (April 1998): 967–84.

Frederickson, B. L. "What Good Are Positive Emotions?" *Review of General Psychology* 2, no. 3 (September 1998): 300–319.

——, and M. F. Losada. "Positive Affect and the Complex Dynamics of Human Flourishing." *American Psychologist* 60, no. 7 (October 2005): 678–86.

——, R. A. Mancuso, C. Branigan, and M. M. Tugade. "The Undoing Effect of Positive Emotions." *Motivation and Emotion* 24 (2000): 237–58.

Frey, Bruno S. "Happy People Live Longer." *Science* 331, no. 6017 (February 4, 2011): 542–43.

Frith, Christopher D., and Daniel M. Wolpert. *The Neuroscience of Social Interac-*

tion: *Decoding, Imitating, and Influencing the Actions of Others*. Oxford: Oxford University Press, 2003.

Gonzaga, Gian C., Rebecca A. Turner, Dacher Keltner, Belinda Campos, and Margaret Altemus. "Romantic Love and Sexual Desire in Close Relationships." *Emotion* 6, no. 2 (May 2006): 163–79.

Gross, J. J. "The Emerging Field of Emotion Regulation: An Integrative Review." *Review of General Psychology* 2 (1998): 271–99.

Handbook of Positive Psychology. Edited by C. R. Snyder and Shane J. Lopez. Oxford: Oxford University Press, 2005.

Hassin, Ran R., James S. Uleman, and John A. Bargh, eds. *The New Unconscious*. Oxford: Oxford University Press, 2005.

Hatfield, E., and R. Rapson. "Love and Attachment Processes." In *Handbook of Emotions*. Edited by M. Lewis and J. M. Haviland, 595–604. New York: Guilford Press, 1993.

Izard, Carroll E. "Basic Emotions, Relations amongst Emotions, and Emotion-Cognition Relations." *Psychological Review* 99 (1992): 561–65.

Jones, James W. *Contemporary Psychoanalysis and Religion*. New Haven, CT: Yale University Press, 1991.

Konner, Melvin. *The Evolution of Childhood: Relationships, Emotion, Mind*. Cambridge, MA: Harvard University Press, 2010.

Larsen, Jeff T., A. Peter McGraw, and John T. Cacioppo. "Can People Feel Happy and Sad at the Same Time?" *Journal of Personality and Social Psychology* 81, no. 4 (October 2001): 684–96.

LeDoux, J. E. "Emotion: Clues from the Brain." *Annual Review of Psychology* 46 (1995): 209–33.

Rychalk, Joseph E. *In Defense of Human Consciousness*. Washington DC: American Psychological Association, 1997.

Schacter, Daniel L. *Searching for Memory: The Brain, the Mind, and the Past*. New York: Basic Books, 1996.

Stern, Daniel N. *The Interpersonal World of the Infant*. New York: Basic Books, 1985.

———. *The Present Moment in Psychotherapy and Everyday Life*. New York: W. W. Norton, 2009.

Wallace, B. Alan. *The Taboo of Subjectivity: Toward a New Science of Consciousness*. Oxford: Oxford University Press, 2000.